The Oval Portrait

The Oval Portrait

Contemporary
Cuban women writers and artists

Originally published as
El retrato ovalado

Edited by
Soleida Ríos

Translated by
Margaret Randall

WingsPress

San Antonio, Texas
2018

First (English) Edition
ISBN: 978-1-60940-557-1 (paperback original)

E-books:
ePub: 978-1-60940-558-8
Mobipocket/Kindle: 978-1-60940-559-5
Library PDF: 978-1-60940-564-9

Wings Press
627 E. Guenther
San Antonio, Texas 78210
Phone/fax: (210) 271-7805
On-line catalogue and ordering:
www.wingspress.com

Wings Press books are distributed to the trade by
Independent Publishers Group
www.ipgbook.com

Library of Congress Cataloging-in-Publication Data:

Names: Râios, Soleida, 1950- editor. | Randall, Margaret, 1936- translator.
Title: The oval portrait / Contemporary Cuban women writers and artists,
 originally published as El retrato ovalado; edited by Soleida Rios;
 translated by Margaret Randall.
Other titles: Retrato ovalado. English.
Description: First edition. | San Antonio, Texas : Wings Press, 2018. |
 Identifiers: LCCN 2017041637 (print) | LCCN 2017045417 (ebook) | ISBN
 9781609405588 (ePub Ebook) | ISBN 9781609405595 (Mobipocket/Kindle)
 ISBN 9781609405649 (Library PDF) | ISBN 9781609405571 (trade pbk. :
 alk. paper)
Subjects: LCSH: Short stories, Cuban--Translations into English. | Cuban
 fiction--21st century--Translations into English. | Cuban fiction--Women
 authors.
Classification: LCC PQ7386.5.E5 (ebook) | LCC PQ7386.5.E5 .R48 2018 (print)
 DDC 863/.01089287097291--dc23
LC record available at https://lccn.loc.gov/2017041637

Contents

Woman will find the unknown!
Will her world of ideas differ from ours?
She will discover strange things, unfathomable,
 repugnant, delicious;
we will gather them up, understand them.

Arthur Rimbaud to Paul Demeny
"Prose on the Coming of Poetry"
Charleville, May 15, 1871

Translator's note

It was a humid, sea-sprayed afternoon in Havana, October 2016, and the launch of *Only the Road / Solo el camino,* my anthology of eight decades of Cuban poetry, had just ended at Casa de Las Américas. My old friend Soleida Ríos handed me a copy of *El retrato ovalado,* a compendium she had put together a few years earlier, then gave me a hug and disappeared into the crowd. When I got home from that trip and opened the book, I knew I held a treasure. When I mentioned it to other Cuban friends, they told me I was fortunate to have a copy. Like so many editions of books on the island, a large print run had sold out almost immediately.

Before reaching the last page, I knew I wanted to translate it. I wrote to Soleida and she agreed. But this English rendition almost didn't happen. On more than one occasion I almost gave up. Finding appropriate English voices for Cuban women who were already writing in another's voice presented complex challenges. These voices within voices, stories within stories, present a rich weave of Cuban culture across centuries. Women—real and imagined, evoked or intended—speak from diverse social classes, races, and historic moments. Some of these writers have chosen to express themselves in the embodiment of women and men from beyond Cuba's borders: Alice in Wonderland, the first woman to summit Mount Everest, Hypatia of Alexandria, or one of South America's "disappeared" of the 1970s. They do so with astonishing guile. But others give us the very Cuban images of a beloved transvestite, a heroine of the country's Independence War, or the first female Cuban filmmaker. Some find inspiration in figures who cross every border, such as the sexually abused young woman who hides behind her protective weight, a woman who puts up with anything for lust or another who gives up a life of excitement in the metropolis to settle into comfortable small town love.

My challenge was to capture voices, social classes, racial characteristics, vernacular. To probe women writing themselves as other

women or as men. As suicided poets, an artist's body finding death out a high-rise window, a painter recreating past in present. To cross borders, the water-lapped shores of an island, time zones of courage. I am immensely glad I stuck it out.

Thank you, Soleida, and thank you to each of the women writers in this anthology. I am also grateful, as always, to Wings Press editor Bryce Milligan, who became as excited about this book as I am. In an era of special interest media and superficial travelogue, I believe *The Oval Portrait* offers readers a uniquely profound glimpse of the Cuban psyche.

—Margaret Randall
Albuquerque, New Mexico
August 2017

To be read in solitude:
an introductory note

Soleida Ríos

Thirty-seven women undress ... but this isn't a striptease.

The performance is open to the public, the game takes us deep.

Each begins by choosing a mask. With it she spins her story and in that story her own image appears as well as the connection (always mysterious) and the symbol with which she's chosen to represent herself.

This conclave (collusion) does not dissemble in struggle: neither universal suffrage and other civil rights, nor those assemblies (so common in Cuba during the second half of our twentieth century) at which household appliances were distributed. We have our voter registration cards. We have received, according to quota, our pressure cookers and rice makers.

> Why are we here?
> Is this really an assembly?
> What do we want?
> Where are we going?
> Are we one?
> Do we have a voice?
> Are we becoming weaker?
> Do we sacrifice ourselves?
> Do we separate ourselves from the Whole?

WE THINK AND LOVE. I allude to Hannah Arendt-Lizabel Mónica. Our fervent desire: TO FIND OURSELVES. Reina María Rodríguez / Marina Tsvetáyeva is speaking.

In order to be able to read this book in solitude, I brought together thirty-four women. Black, white, blue and one or another scarlet

red; old and middle-aged and a good number of young ones. I haven't assembled them randomly, but with every intention. They don't represent any particular group, or literary genre or pre-established aesthetic line. On the list are a lawyer, a philologist, a choreographer, a film critic, a mixed-media artist, a professor, a producer, an editor ... most are writers, especially poets. I've sought this diversity and celebrate it.

I asked each author for a five- to seven-page text, autobiographical in nature, written in another's voice, that is to say, in the voice of a literary or artistic figure from any era and place, or a real person from the pages of universal history. Barring exceptions (insubordinations), that is what I received and have arranged here. Innumerable private conversations were needed to explain my request, guaranteeing a more personal exercise.

The idea took root in me (already in the 1980s I'd done something similar with *Poesía infiel*, a selection of work by young Cuban women poets), and so perhaps it was logical to expect a certain result, a fruit. But that's not what happened, for life is not like that. This greater gift has been the surprise. It is what I offer.

One personage (Woman IX in the text "Exercising the productive...") quotes Dante: *In every act the initial intention of the one engaging in it is to reveal his (her) own image.*

Magnificent! We ask ourselves: what moves us, what determines our choice of that other voice in which we will carry out our experiment, our exercise of conscience?

The game requires us to go deep.

The writer Georgina Herrera, herself something of a heroic figure, chooses Mariana Grajales (19[th] century heroine, mother of the Maceo brothers). She forgives her, and calls her Mother of the Nation.

Adelaida de Juan, well-known art critic, chooses a painting by the expressionist painter Antonia Eiriz. What does she find in that fabulous canvas to put in the artist's mouth?

Adriana Normand reconstructs the (voluntary?) fall from a New York skyscraper by the Cuban painter Ana Mendieta and, even more important, the cloud that hangs over it.

Film critic Azucena Plasencia brings us Cuba's first woman film-

maker Sara Gómez, her mouth filled with the question: *Are we in the future now?*

Alicia, Momo, María Moñitos, Sleeping Beauty (*sleeping so deeply that my dream is my vigil*). The mountain climber Junko Tabei at the top of the world; Hypatia, that enigmatic Greek philosopher; the voices of Alma Rubens and Virginia Woolf's vanished voice; La Giraldilla; Calvert Casey finally with naked shoulders, pearl necklace and two-toned heels descending the staircase of the Asturian Club...; Belkis Ayón, the artist who has given precious iconography to the Abakuá religious sect, still shooting straight and with smoking gun in hand; more and other memories of the poet Juana Borrero; even the self-presentation (file card) of that battered and beaten being who recognizes herself as being without a country.... All are perfect vehicles for introspection.

Shall we say: *Rather than a portrait, construct a mirror, through which you may touch the difficult and shared places*, as Sandra Ramy does in "My Work is You." And then, at the end, ask yourself the question: *Which are your favorite lies?*

S.R.
Havana, August 2012.

The Oval Portrait

Jamila Medina Ríos

Beehive in a Dress of Little Ovals, or, Calvert Casey finally descending the stairs at the Asturian Club, with bare shoulders and a pearl necklace

1

In an alley at dawn or beneath the promenade's evening lights; rowing a boat—her scarf just so—; walking barefoot along the shore; stacking knick-knacks on the market shelf; expectant, watching the traffic light for a chance to cross the avenue (like in a video clip), while she wipes the edge of one hand on the leg of her jeans ... a young girl with her dress of little ovals. Vocalizing on the material: silent portraits; caricatures, cenotaphs, movie stills, a few scandalous flashes and the crayon drawings and news clippings on a bulletin board; little ovals or raw egg mask/shell, parentheses in which, as if caged, a series of birth and death dates sparkle. It is about those gargles, those vocal exercises ... that I wish to speak.

2

During Flora's life, and before and after, modest bodies of every shape seethed and multiplied. Brief skirts, a corset, an embroidered shawl. Waiting on those balconies facing the street, their elbows resting on satin cushions, quiet, at the thresholds of important histories (first communion, marriage, birth, funeral wake). Or, if lucky, escaping on horseback; or wearing a nurse's cap in the hills, if not drunk ... in the warm rags of illness.

Situated in parks, in automobiles, or on a prayer stool in the little church, spying on the entourage. Like a backdrop, an island coat,

stagecraft, with naked breast, dispelling the heat and calling for release (from all that which was inherited, the hero, the knight; the altar boy and scissors-grinder). A vignette, a medallion in the matchmaker's album; footlights, drunken mouth, when provoking pleasure, crime, in the chaste one's breast.

And what do you say about the "Russians" and other worthless foreign women, impoverished queens, selling their nascent flesh, their burnt flesh, their flaccid flesh of meager family legacy. And what about their dreams of going back across the sea, hindered only by isolation's empty bank accounts.

<center>3</center>

From classic antiquity, the mouths of mythic women have gone up in flames. Sacrificed: Iphigenia, wisp of smoke above all those prows of ships headed for Troy; Polyxena, knifed on Achilles' tomb and soon descending to be with him; Cassandra, biting her tongue, prophecy hanging from the thin thread of her voice; Hecuba claiming her children's bodies bristling with spears; Clytemnestra emptied of Agamemnon, walking proud on purple earth; Jocasta and Phaedra, their throats crisscrossed by trembling braids; Medea, the avenger, hostess of fiery feasts, organizer of chaos.

Crisp figures make a commotion on tissue-thin pages, they rise: Judith's brow and chipped sword (General Holofernes' marrow staining her breast). Esther's chin at Purim. Rizpah's scarecrow shriek. Mary Magdalene's dangerous ointments, trading eternity for a bouquet of valerian root....

What do we know about Ophelia's clothes: did they bury her wet in her unwrinkled dress? And what about that sebaceous soap, the gold-plated washbowls where Lady Macbeth scrubbed the palms of her hands in the dimly lit shadows? And what of Lolita's pointed knees, Cinderella's blisters, the vaginal secretions of the unequaled Clawdia Chauchat? What about Wendy's leap from bed, Sleeping Beauty's breath, or Scheherazade's stress, unable to sleep until she could imagine her next day's story.

My grandmother in photos still scattered about: little Cuca who later became a librarian and general—my grandfather's breast heavy with medals for enduring her fights all those years—. My aunts in the album: aunt Irma and aunt Emma who were schoolteachers, one a smoker, the other unmarried, the curmudgeon and the one who circled Cuba several times, still unaware of what awaited her country or her old age (an ischemia, one fourth of the potatoes packed with ghosts, a niece looking for those erotic photographs she glimpsed in a drawer).

My mother's hand in the torrent of sugarcane pulp, shaking out Saturday's laundry, the same gesture with which she said goodbye forever to the tall wooden house and the piano, to the military post and the organ she played at church. In the pleasant smell of the laboratories of my life, the pads of my mother's fingers lightly pinched between the boards, heaven-blue and fuscia hued, so she could glimpse the beauty of adoration and gangrene, homeostasis and ruin.... Under the microscope, a seething, an echo that gives me back my face: feverish with death, testifying bloods, giving difficult birth to monsters.

Standing lazily before the classroom, half smiling in the photos, her gaze on some lost point at the back of the room (on the wall), fan in hand, and the coral of her tongue fixed on fountain-waterfalls, covering herself with that fan, as if protected by a lace shawl: my dance teacher. She forces me into a *pas de deux* of words, to the *jeu d'echecs* of the white page, controlling the zigzag of my *zunzún*. She herself loved twirling. Dragonfly detached from that wise pin, she escaped through water one day, her wings wet, leaving her ship in port, and the border of her pulse like a frieze in my diaries.

<div align="center">5</div>

The witches before their Renaissance spectacle, sinking delightedly in the shadowy marshes. Joan of Arc long before she was scorched in the fire; Charlotte Corday at communion, in her dress

of lilies. Marie Antoinette in the yellow pages of that Stefan Zweig biography crushed beneath my mattress; fragments of the diary in which Elizabeth Bathory wrote less about what she did or saw than what she felt ... Coco Chanel with two slices of cucumber covering her eyes, when she didn't yet know mallow had changed the world; the skin of the serpent who bit Cleopatra, barely enough for the lacing of a single shoe; and Mae West chewing on that phrase of hers: *Is that a gun in your pocket, or are you just glad to see me?*

6

Saint Theresa when she was no longer able to believe. Hildegarde Von Bingen, when she awoke in her bed imagining the letters in which she would talk to God, shortly before she wrote: *What has befallen me / that I am no longer myself? / You drank the substance of my mind.* And all mysticism's other scandalously hot paragraphs written by women: its long unhidden string of purple onions: Hadewijch de Amberes, Margarita Ebner, Gertrudis de Nivelle, María de Oignier, Ida de Lovaina, Margarita de Ypres, Beatriz de Tienen, Gertrude More, Juliana de Mont-Cornillon, Eva de San Martín, Catalina de Siena.... Happy hearts with no need to correct the weakness of a sorcerer's marriage. Lost in the garden's dark night, watering their blood with wine. Devoured/devouring, full of flattery, crazy to attend the hubris of the peacock's fanned tail ...

7

And what can you tell me about the dead hypocrites? Alejandra Pizarnik, little frog at the bottom of a well; and Djuna Barnes in the glades of night; and Sylvia Plath, the ostrich with her head between the oven's legs; and Unica Zürn's mannequin, waiting for dusk in the store windows, unblinking so as not to ruin the photos; and María Luisa Milanés, her mouth a jumble of little blue bells that didn't let her breathe. Sweethearts of madness, they spit; they do not let the pale roses of their mouths be painted with rouge. Cricket green, aqua,

tantrum green, sugarcane green, phlegm green, mucus green, plum marmalade green.... They are splendid, not the cowardly color of the root but the eaten away of bronze and silver, the scourge of iron.

<center>8</center>

Wendy (still William) learning how to polish the silver and sew in the doorways of Vedado, so Ignacio will love him. Wendy, her sex shamelessly disrupted on clinical green, leaving classic drops of blood on the tiles. Matchmaker, seamstress, staring at the handle of the broken sword: Wendy prior to that August 13th, 2011 in La Vana, the first day she applied the necessary lubricant to her new basket, as if on an elegant loving cup.

Ganymede and those other happy adolescent youths: classical antiquity again, eager to study philosophy, ready to experience whatever....

The few boyfriends in my life who painted their lips in front of me, whether with cocoa balm or to write an erotic story. And he who traded his trousers for my denim skirt, and he who tried on my panties, and he who wore my falsies.

Calvert Casey, the Bald Lady, divine and stuttering Leocadia: her four hairs pulled back with an elegant comb, shoulders naked at last, legs sheathed in nylons, body decked out in silk, and around her neck the pearl choker so long embedded on her dual body's tongue. Denied the arm of Giovanni Losito, eternal Italian lover. Casey descending the staircase of the Museum of Universal Art, without stammering, without tripping in her two-tone heels: emerald green and melon-heart red. I know her age, her obsessions, her fears and delights, but I don't care. I know (I have learned it well) the fate of my grandmother and her aunts, the fate of Maria and my mother, the blossoms of mythical women and women poets, of female warriors, of weak women and of the famous. My head shaved so as not to intimidate her with my abundant hair. I have filed my nails. I've visited my psychoanalyst. I have dressed quickly in the manner of these times, I button my jacket and make myself comfortable. I look to another

twist of the screw. More joyous than Lazaro's lover, waiting for him on the skirts of the magic mountain, wearing my most elegant dress, I review my widowhood and *fatum*. I kneel and declare myself at last. I have never asked for or been denied a hand on the staircase or a trio.

Azucena Isabel Plasencia

Sara

(General view. Yolanda and Mario walk away through city streets. They are arguing, each trying to convince the other: what is real, what they believe. On a boom, the camera takes in an aerial view: Mario and Yolanda lose themselves in the noisy atmosphere of the neighborhood. They are gone. We hear the first timid applause rising to ovation. The theater's darkness slowly pales ... to total illumination. The audience remains on its feet for several minutes, whistling, clapping, rhythmically stamping its feet.... There's no way they didn't love it!)

SARA: Are we already in the future? These seem like the same gestures, the same words....

X: Ladies and gentlemen, let the discussion begin. Let's talk about the film....

XX: The first thing I want to say is that Sara Gómez, a refined and well-educated black woman, tried to relegate the intellectual French pose she might have assumed and *tried to be a better person.* That's Mario's and Yolanda's problem: I mean he must overcome a lot of prejudice, a lot of religious and racial fears, taboos that Yolanda the teacher has already put behind her.

XY: What attracts me about this film, what interests me, is how the director focuses in on and shows us the reality of her time: unaltered, without distortions. REALITY. With its lights and shadows. Its virtues and miseries. Without rhetoric. Naked. This isn't a work of art.... (We hear exclamations of disagreement, booing.) It's not a

work of art, I repeat: it's Life, it's these times, it's affirmation and commitment.... The director is able to portray us as we have been, as we are, with our contradictions, our systemic intolerances. She wants Mario to rid himself of the secular customs that prevent him from moving forward with the Revolution that belongs to everyone. Remember: we're talking about the seventies....

XXY: A French pose, you say. So, we are talking about an existential problem. This film is anthropological, sociological, it searches for the origins of human behavior. Those marginal people of Las Yaguas upon whom she trains her cameras and lights, those she allows to see the 16 millimeter rushes fresh from the lab, so she can film their reactions, the sides they take.... It's very important, comrades: that they take sides, because those marginal people are still to be found among us, after fifty years of a Revolution based on Martí and on Marx. The same or worse gestures and terms; the same spiritual smut: opportunism, delinquency, apathy, negligence..."qualities" that have increased sevenfold!

X. Please, let's get back to analyzing the film, no more speeches....

SARA: Are we already in the future? Existential problem, you say? It's just sincerity, tenacity, honesty: the only way one could conceive of making a film. To express my opinion, my way of seeing things. To impose oneself, not give in, not make concessions, especially when you know you're right (or mostly right). Film, for me, will always inevitably be partial, the product of a particular attitude when considering the problems we are faced with as revolutionaries. When we confront the need to decolonize ourselves politically and ideologically, to "break with traditional values," whether economic, ethical or aesthetic.

That's why I filmed my family first: a chronicle, a portrait of an era, of a lifestyle that was destined to disappear because of the whirlwind that is the Revolution. Then I filmed youth from all over the country, gathered on Isle of Pines, that other island. Not much more than children, they belonged to a work and study contingent: they

were pioneers in the State's strategic plan of holistic education, or what we called "the formation of the new man." They sat in the fields, beneath the morning sun, to squish earthworms upended by tractor wheels. In the afternoons, in their classrooms, they literally fell asleep at their desks, exhausted by such unproductive agricultural work.... Many tried to escape by boat—Treasure Island, the Jigüe—rotting coastal ferries, to get back to their provinces, their homes, *their family*. Most of them stole food in the noisy dining hall with its shrieking tin trays. Before the camera, they mouthed slogans or simply stuttered, spewing half-formed sentences. They also spoke a few truths. To which no one listened.

In short, we are in a transitional period, one concerned with trying to change a society of injustice and discrimination for one that promises equality in a better world. Observing Life. Documentary and fiction. *De cierta manera* looks at the residents of Miraflores, a place built for those who once lived in Las Yaguas. They are helped to see their problems, to confront them. There is that mother with her child who is behind at school; without help from his family he won't pass to the next grade, we understand it's not just up to the teacher. They were very damaged people, with all their 19th century rituals, subject to social contempt. I wanted to establish a bridge between the different images on the screen and the REALITY I was referencing. The social environment, its complex mix. Yes, we did have to fight against material and spiritual poverty, against sexism! There was so much to do....

ASSISTANT TO THE DIRECTOR: Germinal, where is Sara?

GERMINAL: Over there, trying to breathe: she's having a bad asthma attack! There's a lot of humidity, cold...and then, so much dust!

SARA: Go out, out into the street. They are tearing down walls: it's a world that is disintegrating. Close-up on the boy's eyes: what a tough look, it rips your heart out! We're going to film the workers' assembly in a broad shot, then a medium-range shot moving to Mario seated among the others. Let's keep that American-style shot when Alberto

explains himself, when he makes his self-criticism before his comrades. He lies. Medium-range shot. Cut. Go on to the workers' faces. Close-up. Which take is that?

ECOBIO I: That's not a manly thing.

ECOBIO II: No lack of respect either.

ECOBIO I: Rat! Twit! Never that!

ASSISTANT TO THE DIRECTOR: Germinal, where is Sarah?

SARA: Okay, Tomás, let's cut to the ritual scene, to Ilocha's house.... Show us their Fambá room...the Náñigo rite...just a few shots, very discrete. We must be respectful of their beliefs. Only what they want us to see!

ASSISTANT TO THE DIRECTOR: Sara! Sara!

SARA: Music? Let's ask Sergio Vitier. But even better that neighborhood musician, singing his own work. Mortal!

GERMINAL: Her asthma is going to kill her...

XXY: It's a love story, of friends, of betrayed loyalties. *De cierta manera* is, above all, a reaffirmation of the collective imagination, of people who want to make themselves better...

XX: Documentary and fiction, mixed messages: this is a film for those who are conscious of the social place in which they live.... But films are above all spectacles.... The director should speak *from that sense of marginality*, not expound upon it....

SARA: Are we already in the future? There are so many movies to make! Sometimes I experience my profession as a challenge and a

privilege. To express the contradictions, the achievements of men and women capable of looking at life in eternal conflict with what surrounds them.... Am I being too ambitious?

ASSISTANT TO THE DIRECTOR: Sara! Sara!

Caridad Atencio

Clouds Within / Clouds Out There

The island had become a part of our breath. Someone already said that. I always think about how different points of view are articulated: physical, metaphysical, contextual. I think of the tyranny of place; that place where we raise ourselves up and simultaneously prevents us from growing. That's how starting and stopping ourselves confuse us in dreams.

I said somewhere, referring to another poet—a reading I can't forget—that people perceive fences on the social grid where popular philosophy is the same as judgement, judgement the same as custom, custom the same as aspiration, and all this is circumscribed by eco-nomics. The writer always describes one configuration and proposes another, or presents them in a combat in which systems and ambigui-ties are all mixed up. Multidimensional, ubiquitous, life threatens you. I've written a book about our relationship to language, where I reclaim the nuclear condition for that literary framework of whatever dimen-sion: *The explosion and its nullification/misrepresentation in the question. The explosion and its nullification/misrepresentation in the answer.* And so: *A book—for me, made by me—is the journey of consciousness through a certain state.* Disintegrating fiber or shredded thread. Or nouns as adjectives. Crypt with a view of the sky: the reduction and abuse of the photo. Poetry hides half of what it wishes to reveal. It is in that struggle that one is surprised, and the journey—the explosion—begins again. To presuppose a weave, a grid in a certain sense preceded by a variety of questions is, at the very least, an impossible effort. Because we leave our lost footprint everywhere we go, these lines and their extenuating circumstances are revealed in everything we've written. By asking you've already organized the answers.

I don't know how I also began to transform myself into an island, tired of containing the constant explosion of waves washing over me. I traded the scars I kept for fear and anxiety. As I always wanted to hide the world in my breast, I went out to receive *anguish become destiny—and instead of wisdom—experience, insipid drink that does not quench one's thirst.* On one trip, when still an adolescent, I understood I had died, and that events repeated themselves like mechanical branches of trees, always ready to begin again. And I live with the obsession, examining and preaching. To be at a loss will chisel my body. The Carmelite nun brands me with her life's excision: *Everything trembles in me, whether rigid or lax,* with the false saltiness of my suit and the bloodstain they erased. We mend the fissure with thick ropes and sharp spikes surrounding the body and wounding it at times, making of mine a parallel body that imprisons it, that frightens it. I rely upon myself. That erases everything. My dress's white train unravels as I walk, even as it carries all that I have destroyed.

Laura Ruiz Montes

Half an Hour on the Summit

It is May 16, 1975, and I am at the top of the world. In my pocket my hand squeezes the bouquet of little pine boughs tied with white paper ribbons. I come from the easternmost extreme of the Silk Road and I am—oh my God!—at the top of the world.

I made it. I don't know if I will be able to sustain the camera and my leg hurts a bit, but I made it. The *Sherpa* looks at me as if he knows exactly what hurts me most. But no, he doesn't know, he just looks at me. Contemplates me. Contemplates the mound of clothing that covers me and asks himself, silently, if beneath those layers I am like his brother's wife, who is also his.

I still remember his face when we met. I said Junko Tabei and he observed me for a few moments before bowing courteously, respectful and skeptical. I squeezed the little pine boughs so I could feel that all the *kamis* were with me. Only then, in the delicate whisper of his eastern traveler's dialect, did he say his: Ang Tsering.

Now, on the summit, Tsering looks at me. I know what he is thinking. He is asking himself if under all that clothing there really is a woman. It can't be, isn't possible that there is. A woman has never made it to the top of the world. China, Nepal, Tibet...they've never been beneath a woman's feet. The *Sherpa* never imagined he would see Everest dominated in this way.

The lack of oxygen pressure is what turns the farthest mountains indigo. Brushing those indigo mountains and those snow-capped mountains are fistfuls of dark earth. I myself am a dark speck against those white peaks. In the midst of such whiteness, if I undressed my body would be the color of the houses of Nagasaki that Kipling saw, *the color God gave wood.*

I am thirty-six years old. Thirty-six like the thirty-six views of Mount Fuji that Hokusai painted and printed. Hokusai, dreamed of by Van Gogh. Fuji dreamed of by all the women denied its summit. I went to Mount Fuji and climbed it, knowing it was the highest peak in the Empire of the Rising Sun. I myself became one of its folds, one of Mount Fuji's peaks. Sacred as it, like it an active volcano. And like it, of scant threat, with little risk of erupting.

I have followed the path of Edmund Hillary and Tenzing Norgay: the South Face route, from Nepal where some children asked me if it was true that I would climb to the sky's forehead. It is May, the most appropriate moment. The moment before the monsoons, before the rains soak that forehead, the face of the mother mountain of the universe.

We've been in the death zone for hours. And something in addition to myself, has agonized as the climb progressed. The earth is dying. I ascended and the earth bowed down until it was small, waning, an old woman diminished and bent. This is the zone where it is no longer possible to acclimate yourself, almost the point of no return.

I have had to draw fifteen breaths each time I took a step. Fifteen, like Benedict and his new canonical code. Fifteen, like Carlos, king of Sweden. Fifteen, like Gregory when he canonized Saint Ignatius Loyola. Fifteen like Louis, accepting advice from the marchioness of Pompadour. Fifteen breaths before moving again. Like with great decisions: breathe deeply and then make your move, without knowing exactly what you will find.

At times I have felt my head oscillate from side to side, from Fukushima to the Matterhorn. And like the Matterhorn become a pyramid, become several lateral faces and in each of them a mountain. That's the altitude sickness, confusing vertex with vertigo. A voice speaking in Quechua, foreign like myself, explaining this Sickness of the Mountain, explaining it to me, this Sickness of the Heights, this Wellness of Life.

Katmandu was the first. *Nepal with no outlet to the sea,* as the cruel childhood ditty goes. And like Buddha, I too am born—again—in Nepal. The white cupolas of Bodnath prepare me for the flashes

of snow. There an ancient nun asked me if I was going to the sky's forehead. But she did not wait for my answer. She disappeared, heading toward her stupa. I remained motionless for a long time, learning the art of respiration. Searching for focus in the pastime of imagining the noise of the trains that run from Kathmandu to India. Immobile, breathing, readying myself to be able to survive in the Valley of Silence. Trying on silence surrounded by Kathmandu's concert of horns, as I was being tossed about by the noise. The wisdom of that which moves, the reality of everyday life...and there, unexpectedly, without announcing itself, my moment of doubt arrived. A coldness in my soul, a desire to go home, a *mal de coeur*.

Rest days enabled me to retrieve the notion of colors and many other sensations. The blood red tents, the mustard colored blankets faded by time. The colorless wind, rising and falling, falling and rising. Conversations with other climbers were marked by our voices disconnected from our thoughts and our permanent, nerve-wracked desire to reach the summit.

Camping and our time at Base Camp made us feel like exiles. *Homeless* and radish-colored and in danger of dying in the first avalanche. *Clochards* in crab-like tones, biting our own teeth, thinking of the next journey across the Ice Field. We all pretended to be in the same sweet and sour sauce, but we knew the loose rocks held danger: softness promised death. The summit possibility separated the ingredients in that sauce. Some would achieve the sweet pain of reaching the top. Others, bitterness served up on plates of burnt lacquer, the final question of whether there really was a better place to die.

I am at the top of the world. I practice correctly pronouncing George Everest's name. I studied the English language so I would be able to do so, so I would be able to say George Everest correctly and so the letters' sounds would overcome the atrocious sound of the wind. I learned the language to make a pilgrimage into Chaucer. To learn from Dickens that *it was the epoch of incredulity, it was the season of Light, it was the season of Darkness, it was the spring of hope, it was the winter of despair....* And not to forget that today *was the best of times.*

In less than twenty years I will complete the Seven Summits. I will climb Kilimanjaro moved by my initiation into the black coffee growing on its flanks. I will be a stoic stone sentinel on Aconcagua. I will adore the purity of graphite in the Caucasus, and I will repeat until I am delirious the beautiful sound of *Tbilisi, Tbilisi, Tbilisi.*

It is May 16, 1975 and I am—Oh my God!—at the top of the world. Soon I will have to begin my descent, but at this moment, in this eternal hour, I am truly only ten years old and I squeeze the little pine boughs between my fingers as I arrive atop Mount Nasu with my professor. There, trembling, exalted, I think all this is better than greeting the imperial family twice a year. Better than traveling the entire Silk Road on a camel. Better than the love between the celebrated dancer Hanko and Rodin.

And I know, from this moment on—and it is the only thing I will ever really know—that my center isn't the line that runs from my navel to my coccyx, but the interminably long distance that goes from this white summit and Collado's tone to my childhood medulla, immature, conquering yet virgin.

Nara Mansur

I Am Not Sleeping Beauty

He kisses me with lips that are a bit moist and awake. At last he's awake—I tell myself. At last I can change all this. I don't know if it's the first thing I think or remember. Is it a dream, a beautiful dream or the immense absence of that event in my life? And these lips that kiss me and this moistness that brushes me like a creed, and this man, who is he, who pretends to wake me after years of hunger, following my isolation, my despair?

Here is the spinning wheel: what have I been able to learn? Have I learned enough so they will recognize me (the princess with the spinning wheel beside her in the brightly colored photograph)? I walk to the spinning wheel: what a strange artifact, I don't sing, nor do I pinch myself anew. I'm not Sleeping Beauty then. I have no name. I am not me.

(Pause.)

I am not going to be that woman they expected me to be: she of the strawberry lips, of eyes like pearls, the one who shows up in Puerto Argentino carrying bags filled with breads and fishes. No. Not any longer. The Sleeping Beauty that I am, or might be, the sleeping beauty I am not, I'm not sure, or perhaps I will be one day in the company of a man dreaming me even now. The little figure in the story wakes up, she is up and takes a shower as romantic as it is tepid, and what do I do? I cry and say: I want my mother and father, I want to be with them. And the prince, what does he do, what does he say? He is afraid, my tenderness is erotic, and he consoles himself thinking I am truly asleep, that it's something internal, something you can't

see; no one sees the sleeping beauty's words, those words that do not describe her, that do not accompany her in any of history's versions. How embarrassing.

But I am awake or rather, I sleep so soundly that my sleep is my vigil. I wait, just wait for the kiss that will carry me even further into the unknown, that will permit me to surf my stigmata. I stay here for a few moments and think of those objects I left some time before, when the needle pierced the pad of my finger, when that apparently inoffensive prick sent me into another world: that of the insomnia of closed eyes, of unachievable love, of voluntary work.

I am the pioneer at Pioneer Palace, the palace where we plant the shimmering red tree that doesn't shimmer, the red tree no Havana wind can move. I arrive there like the little girl you are, with small pearls in my ears, with some worn book after having kissed the hero on the television screen.

> The pioneer palaces are more important than the pioneer camps. The pioneer palaces are as important or more important than the primary and secondary schools. And our system of education won't be complete until we have a pioneer palace in every city and municipality in the country.

> *(Applause.)*

They have invited me to a dance at the Pioneer Palace. Something will happen today, something will change places. He will come with his kiss of spontaneous words, marvelous words unknown to me, or with his biting silence, his savage "here I am." Either possibility will do because I believe both men, those two possible men I can coerce a little from my cry in the shadows. He adores me without even looking. With his strawberry mouth, his rose mouth, with his golden chair, it is hunger's music that causes him to dance. If anyone must come later, let it be the princess.

The princess does not laugh, the princess does not feel. The princess is pale. The princess is sad. I am no less beautiful although I

have a ruffled collar.

The dream has been the same for everyone, we have slept one hundred years in this land of ours, now we will rise to work.

We must work, one hundred years asleep and the land unravels in infertility; we must milk the cows; we must go down into the mines to excavate copper and cobalt; we must open the schools, the movie theaters; we must clear a pathway in the forest among wasps and marabou; we must certainly learn to use the spinning wheel.

They count money, we count sleeping bodies, and beautiful stories as well. Scattered bodies of men and animals who seem dead but are only sleeping. They have red noses and congested faces, a few drops of wine remain in their glasses.

Laws aren't justice but we must also write them. That's why the princess doesn't want them to say about her that she seeks the vague dragonfly of vague illusion.

I do not want to be a swallow, I do not want to be a butterfly, I do not love the enchanted hawk or the scarlet buffoon. I am dying of love.

And the little princess sleeps again, gets drunk again, is too hungry to wait for the servants, too sleepy to learn anything at the Pioneer Palace, something that might be useful in times to come. She sleeps, then, alone in her prison, leaving her long golden tresses to the prince.

Teresita Burgos

Perennial Leaves

The tundra was carved for me by the force of its winds. Neither the utter whiteness of its borders nor its mute tombs can touch me. I am the one who never dies, but this doesn't satisfy me.

I see your back bent over the reams, how carefully you cut the paper, your wounded breath.... The silent anguish beneath your clothing might detain me, or the sacrificial wait; nevertheless, I must say: go back! Make me mortal in the mist.

I only wanted his strong embrace, his voice. Return me to a place far from the Lintons, those vanishing hills. Make the sun shine forever.

I have knocked on the windows in the rain and no one has answered. I wander among the heather, in this arid place to which I have been condemned. Yesterday I saw him with frost in his hair, blood flowing from his cheeks. Smoke rose about him and I could not get close. You must destroy my spirit as soon as you can. I am beside you, ready for the event. Don't deposit in me the life that escapes you. Let us be simple leaves, nameless leaves on the wind, fleeing a dusky county.

Bells ring in the distance. I look at my room. Everyone has gone, but he twists in the tempest, freezes waiting to enter. There is nothing I can do. Only lay down. He opens my coffin, kisses my withered body, hugs what I was against his tears. Why this eternity for us? Death and life, life, life, life...inseparable and distant, burning or cold like everything that grows within you.

I still remember when he returned and I languished in the farm's heat. I still see his deep eyes that demolished my calm, the apparent peace of those days that diminished my strength. He made the sword's last thrust in me. It wasn't when I gave birth; it was when I saw him,

believing him to be lost in an emaciated woman. But nothing could sever our invisible bridles.

To die and remain alive in the candlelight where you weave our passions each night. Late night illuminates your eyes as you wait for your brother, as you worry about his indiscretions. When you see him arrive drunk and you wash and dress him, your mind expands and you look for us so you may let go.

Let us save ourselves from becoming solitary ghosts, watching snow fall on the branches of resistant holly, your most cherished symbol. We are the pages that fly toward distant water, wetting the heather.

At your side, I have lived it all and need nothing now. Go back and trace the house without discarding the great sheets of paper wrapped about you. Set me free. Why save the frozen heaths that populate me with such a strange love?

You made him of another stock and were willing to rip me apart. He listened, now I know he heard what I once confessed. He knew of my love, my malicious nature. He went off in search of riches and I was never again the same. His abandonment relegated me to Thrushcross's rooms and I couldn't recover.

Just as your brother destroyed the paintings, so he could raise your indecisive visage, just as your sisters went off forever, you placed your pain in us, and we would never again be together. Only the weight of that time exists when we were innocent inseparable children.

Why was everything so hard? Even at that, we lost. We all lost, although desperation and death have rendered us indelible. We fade in the emptiness that remains. It is what matters. And I feel lost in my condition of errant ghost.

I know that others rest close by, but it is in this exile that you alone can give me what I deserve: oblivion. It might be true death in which no one will recognize me and where he will be able to find me free from the world's pressures.

You have little time left among the living, with the consumption that has always laid in wait for you, but while you live try to see that we have everything. I prefer not to transcend in his love, I prefer not

to break my heart in a sentiment that destroys me and never lets up.

I know you understand me, although you have spent too many nights in vigil and need to calm your doubts and anxieties. You can glimpse his destiny and mine in your own body. Did you accumulate so much that everything was ruined for you? Where is your love? On which cold plain did you see it appear? What other woman stole her breast from you?

You, us: we are the same. We float fused in what only crystalized within you. If you save us from eternity you might die beneath the Yorkshire snow, with someone who didn't arrive in time to kiss the ink on your fingers.

We are your footsteps, two lovers who wander the plains looking to grab onto branches that trace the signs of omens.

Now wind has begun to blow in the gloom. The clouds hang so low we can touch them. He waits for me at the edge of the ravine where everything dissolves. I am going to meet him. Your heart loses its leaves as you watch us disappear.

Damaris Calderón

In the Land of "In Between," Beaten by the Waters

Separate faces live in my face (I remember, I plagiarize). I open my eyes. I wake. Here it is drizzling outside, there it may be raining, but in this no man's land I move only in the *in between*, among the *ins and outs*. Delicate drops fall upon the zinc roof. My dogs sleep. Birds crisscross the morning. I, anonymous poet in a few years, raise my voice with the anonymous pre-Colombian poet singing to the new day's beauties:

> Beauties of the day
> Great Teachers
> Heavenly spirits
> Earthly spirits
> Givers of Yellow
> Givers of Green [...]
> Return to us
> Scatter the Yellow
> ...the Green.[1]

Such an old song, so new, so alive, it can bring together a man and woman separated by centuries and reunite them at the instant of celebration. And this new day also brings you. To eat a little of your yellow, your green, the rosy purple of your nipples, grass, rose, flower, sprig that brushes my lips, immersing you in me.

From my window, I have seen a bird perched on the airy carnation (you on me). A moment, and it is gone. A mad chord.

1 *Poesía precolombina*, selection, introduction and notes by Miguel Angel Asturias, Campañía General Fabril Editora, Buenos Aires, 1960.

Our wooden houses on this other island are another sign of our fragility. *What we see burning.* But Sappho's voice, in the morning, brings me back; it is as powerful as the song of the birds: *I have no complaints/ about the prosperity/ the golden muses/ gave me/ it was no illusion/ death, I will not be forgotten.*

Looking at the sharp-pointed leaves, the carnation's lack of roots, I told him, as if telling myself: "You belong to no one," but this, which might be overconfidence, or simply confidence, is also a certain sadness, an exclusion.

I have made a great pot of pasta, for me and my dogs. The same for us all.

Sometimes I receive messages from Cuba, like messages from another world, from the world of the dead.

The fragile line between reason and madness. I am, at one and the same time, the woodcutter, hangman and fallen tree. And also the leaf carried by the wind, that rises on the wind and disappears.

Virginia Woolf's madness, as if it weren't the madness of an era, world wars, the allies, the bombs, the alienation even if one had *a room of one's own.* Everything so precarious, so fragile, when faced with war, with life. The eagerness for words, to find a language that would express and reconcile that which is human.

You lend me a book about Virginia Woolf, *El vicio absurdo,*[2] and put small white wildflowers that you gathered between its pages. The absurd vice—the writing, the madness, the suicide?—acquires a fragrance, the determination of a flower.

I (too) have devoted my life to the absurd vice.

I am a woman who depends on two dogs, just as earlier I depended on two crutches and on a season: spring, summer, love, waiting for its first blossoms. *But in the depths of love, each of us is alone.* (I remain with the pack.) This flower is called white cardinal and that one blue cardinal and that one over there petunia. Suddenly everything acquires a vegetable cruelty.

2 Viviane Forrester: *Virginia Woolf: El vicio absurdo,* Ultramar Editores, Madrid, 1982.

My poor circus life, the life of a poor circus animal. And the *consecration of poverty* ends with the noose around your neck, the dancing legs of the hanged man or the body sinking in the river, its pockets filled with stones.

(I don't talk to angels, I talk to dogs, equal to equal.)

No introspection. I write down Henry James' phrase: Continually observe. Observe the coming of age. Observe desire. Observe your own oppression. And everything will be of use. At least I hope so. I insist upon taking every advantage of these times. I will go under with my standard raised. I am aware that this borders on introspection, but do not give myself to it entirely. [...] It is essential to keep busy.

And now with a certain delight, I discover it is seven and I must make dinner. Cod and sausage. There is no doubt the cod and sausage acquire a certain elegance when one writes their names.

As I copy Virginia Woolf's words (as I) run to the kitchen, make sure the rice hasn't burned, that the pork is okay, I water the plants, and feed the dogs. Following Virginia, the Zen master and above all a strong survival sense, I try to keep busy, think about things outside myself, not become entangled with the intimate, with *introspection* (the internal procession). I try to keep my distance like the boxer keeps his from his dangerous rival, his adversary who faces him. I try to achieve a bit of order, a bit of calm, so the most absolute solitude may remain absolute.

My god, how I suffer. What a terrible capacity for feeling everything with such intensity [...] How to survive one more year? But people do live. It is impossible to imagine what happens behind a face. Everything is a hard surface. I myself am no more than an organ that receives blows, one after another. And my eyes hurt. And my hands tremble [...] . I really must congratulate this woman who is terribly depressed [...] myself.

This woman through whose head so much pain has passed. Who was sure she had failed. Because, in spite of everything, I think she is better and must be congratulated. I wouldn't know how to say how she achieved that, her head like a rag.

But I don't play at Woolf or at Mistral or at the literary animal. I am what I am and that which is. A body filled with solitude, sadness, mushrooms. A body where solitude grows like mushrooms, like vines, ivy, between darkness and humidity. I think (I write) *humidity* and immediately feel a sticky sensation, nausea, native to the islands, their malignant circularity (here, beside me, the dark bird, like Virgil, the joke, the colossal grimace). And yet, I have never loved anyone like I love the islands, that bland and tasteless mouthful I become when engaged in *the resentful work of remembering*. As awkward as a country, I take my first steps, I cannot stand it, I do not learn to decide. The same old whip, despotic, secondhand mind. Obsession with the mother (the lighthouse) (*To the Lighthouse*) and the waves, always the waves, surging, breaking against the reefs, in my head.

And on the other island, in the remote country, my mother walked with short steps, like a wounded bird, with one knee she couldn't bend, speaking so low you could barely hear her voice, as if she had no strength left, as if she was a candle burning out over the water. (Here I take a step and am always in the *in between*, walking like an orphan, with my mother).

And in the universal images I hear repeated references to Chile, *the England of America*, that other island in local parlance. Chile: That country no one knows where it is. That country where the world ends. That country so far away. That country where it seems so easy to die. And I forget reading. And I forget writing. I forget letters, the alphabet. In a metaphor (Isla Negra) I create another metaphor, a space, a house, a nest, a niche, where I become (convert myself into) the only thing I can: a woman, an island, neither a finished being nor a sharp surface that files its edges: a stone, a mollusk. Not Virginia Woolf, not Emily Dickinson, not Marina Tsvetaeva.

Not Damaris Calderón or D.C., but someone (something) who, dragged by the mud of the word *mud*, sinks in the current to the bottom, devoured by the waters of *the in between*.

Isla Negra, Tuesday, January 29, 2013

For Virginia Woolf, at the moment she achieved
her highest expression in suicide

Amalia Iduate

The Cat

—Hipólito Abril?

—Speaking. Who's this?

—You don't know me, but I'd like to know you.

—Who are you? How did you get this number?

—I don't want to bother you. Talk to me about yourself—he added suddenly.

A pause, then the discouraging reply:

—Please, don't call again.

April is the cruelest month, he thought, smiling, after accepting the unknown person's evasive response. The only thing he knew about Hipólito was his name and address. And hearing his voice made the temptation more real. Verifying Hipólito Abril's existence made him want to know him. Two criteria guided him. He knew absolutely nothing about him. And the sound of his name was very attractive. In less than a minute, the tone of his greeting, question and refusal had revealed a lot about that voice. A photograph is the memory of an image but a voice is the memory of the soul, was something that had once occurred to him.

In his loneliness, he thumbed the pages of the telephone book. It was the most public privacy in print. How many unknown people. How many people. You appear there if you have a telephone and a house. That means five hundred and thirty-five pages in this, the capital city, in 2009. Even then there were so many. A book of people with whom you might communicate. Nothing justifies loneliness now. What made him read it? He was tired of himself. He wanted to be someone else. To imagine himself as another.

You don't choose your name. Others choose it for you. And others, unimaginable others throughout time, your surname. Do you

choose your existence? From time to time. If you could choose another name, would you be choosing another existence? Perhaps. The next thing to do would be go to the civil registry, so he could change his own name to Hipólito. But before that he would explore around his house. See him without being seen. He wasn't yet sure he wanted to know him personally.

In that telephone directory he had discovered extraordinary names. Like Violeta Waterland and Adelina Vegetable. The moment he read her name, Violeta Waterland was wearing a blue silk dress. Adelina managed a restaurant. Without doubt. That mirage was the result of simply having read their names. That mirage ignited and blinded him with enthusiasm. Each name, a life. It's not civil or reasonable to call in order to verify. He took a chance with Hipólito because he found Abril decisive. Is it a crime to call someone again and again? Isn't there some joke about that? Is it a joke to use your telephone for that sort of thing? In the end, I think it's the victims who pay. They are forced to change their numbers. Our high-tech systems can identify calls these days. They know who calls you. They can trace the calls. Technological protection rather than laws.

Why do telephone books exist? Who can answer that, Graham Bell? Telephones are commonplace now. The telephone takes you to a name. And an address. So, let's get to know one another. If you are alone on the Island with a telephone book and a telephone, you're not alone, Robinson. It's as amazing as the fingerprint. Singular and unique anthropological surprise useful to today's criminology. Errorless search. We are unique. A telephone can change owners when they move from one house to another. That was before. And they'd tell you: —No, he doesn't live here anymore. Now you can take your number with you. ETECSA, on line with the world. The world? MODEM: Modulator-Demodulator. It transforms telephonic pulses into electrical signals and vice-versa. A telephone in your *Personal Computer* in order to write, not speak. And so I really do have more world.

Here you can only have one piece of property, so only one tele-phone. Going through the book several times, looking for persons,

personages and personified egos, I only found two brothers with one telephone and the same house. Something unusual in this country. I am guessing they are bothers because they have the same last name and it's not a common one. And if they're not the only ones? Common surnames like Pérez are interesting too. And then there are repetitions of unusual names, such as Aquiles and Evaristo. Several, as a matter of fact.

What is it like in other places? There are inverted guides. When I was in Switzerland, everything so developed, you typed the telephone number into a little electronic machine and it gave you the name. A book in reverse. It's just as well that cell phones don't yet have that. You don't have to have a house to have a cell phone. But now we know about the problem of receiving calls: you must pay for them. You try to defend against them. Please don't print a telephone book for cell phones. Not a good idea. A guide for people who share the AB+ blood type. Who knows? Perhaps, and they'd have more in common for having the same blood type. *Delicatessen* for vampires.

But it's not telephones that interest me. It's names. A book of names of living citizens, neighbors, compatriots, general public. I looked in the telephone book for a name for my son. So many names. I went to another, older, book: the Bible. Where every name has a meaning. Not names for names' sakes. Each thing by its name, and people too. My cabala isn't very complete, but didn't they add numbers, assigning a number to every letter and the sum indicated a fate, and then interpreting and reinterpreting was about inserting yourself into a dissolving universal energy? Ah, those mysteries. Ah, the mystery of forgetting them. The name or the rose? I am interested in the Rose and in Hipólito Abril. Flowers in April.

He approached the house they said belonged to Hipólito. In Central Havana. He checked the number. It was early in the morning and he was surrounded by typical early morning noises. It was on the ground floor. A little house facing the street. Windows closed. Scrubby façade. As he pretended to wait, as he slowly looked around, who did he run into but his friend Frank Mirabal.

—Maaaan! What are you doing here? How many years since

we've seen one another! How are you? Are you still working there?

—Yesssss, therrre—surprised to run into one another, they dragged out syllables and handshakes.

—Want to come in and have a cup of coffee? Come on, old friend. Let me introduce you to my wife. Neither of us is working. We're about to leave.

—You're leaving the country?

—Yes, we're leaving. As a matter of fact, tomorrow we're having a gathering here, just some friends. Maybe one of the last. Why don't you come?

—Rosa, come and meet the Cat, an old friend. Get him some coffee.

—Pleased to meet you—the woman said. And she completed the ritual kiss after handing him the cup.

—Tomorrow night. Some friends are coming over, some who worked there, people you know, but they left that job in disgust. And some family is coming, and neighbors.

—Did you marry?

—Yes, but we're separated. We didn't have children.

—Ah, old friend. Loneliness makes us solitary. But the important thing is to feel good about yourself. Do you know, I don't know your name. I always just called you the Cat, like everyone else.

—Yeah, that's what they call me. You don't want to know my name. My aunt did me a favor by changing it. You should remember me like this. Now that you're leaving, you'll have to learn what to forget and what to remember. I'll always be the Cat to you. If they shouted something else at me in the street, I probably wouldn't turn around....

He'd finished the coffee and stood up, intending to give back the cup and make his way to the door to leave. He wasn't far from the Civil Registry, and that's where he'd planned on going.

—Sure, man, I'll write down my address, be sure to come. Now that you're single, meeting new people is good for you.

—I'll come. You'll see me here on Saturday.

He departed, his heart beating fast. Neighbors are coming? Is

Hipólito invited? What a coincidence!

But, do I want to meet him? Do I want to complete my imagination's image? What will he be like? If I've decided to become him, I should get to know him better. Or at least learn to act like him. People are relaxed and happy at parties. If the alcohol does its minimal job they act almost like they really are. Yes, I'll come. It's a possibility. An opportunity. Coincidences can be fate's alibis, made for and by destiny. Even if only to change it. Destiny is changeable. That's what no one seems to see. I'll go to the party and I'll believe that Abril will be there too. He was thinking all this as he made his way to the Central Civil Registry.

He left dejected. The only real possibility of changing one's name is to change one's gender. And he and Hipólito had the same gender. None of the other possibilities, judicial or administrative, were open to him. If you want to change your name, you must bring documents showing that you are known by another name. Diplomas, certificates. If possible, a witness. If it's your surname, it's a judicial process. Someone who believes his father is his stepfather rather than his biological father, and wants to recognize him in life by changing his last name. A judge decides.

—It's not possible to change your name on a whim—the woman who attended him said. Imagine. Not even your surname. We'd have too many requests on our hands. There are laws. There are limits—and then she got friendlier—. What's the problem? What's your name?

—I can't tell you that yet. I'll know that on Saturday. Or I won't ever know.

They call me the Cat. And this is my seventh life.

Legna Rodríguez Iglesias

I'm Easy and I'm Drunk

I am Momo and I am in control.

I have grown, I have gotten fatter, I've been drinking for hours so I do not have to know where I am. So I do not have to stand up. Hold me up. I have come home the same way I left. Finding curiosities along the way: an arm, a leg, a tuft of hair, some eyes, a piece of nose. Flowers.

I am Momo and I am fatter. I weigh 180 pounds. Even so, I am in control. Of the gray men. Who love me. All of them crazy for me. Slippery as they are. Those men.

Twenty-eight years. That is how old I am. I want to get married. Establish myself. But this fat. Enormous. It robs me of my confidence.

I have boyfriends.

One sits on the curb and thinks about me for a long time until his mother looks out and calls him stupid, why don't you do something worthwhile. Another sits on the curb and thinks about me for a long time until his mother looks out and calls him stupid, why don't you do something worthwhile. Something valuable. Things worth doing. Things that will get you recognition, a diploma covered with signatures and stamps.

I am Momo and I love them. I know that I love them as I sit at the dining room table and think long and hard about all those people who know me ever since *Momo*, the book, was published, until my mother looks into the room and calls me stupid, get up from the table, you're ruining our plans.

I am Momo and I am going for a walk. I am going out. I am going to lose some time since I have nothing more to lose, because I have lost everything I had. I only had one thing and I lost that one thing. Although I am still in control.

I am Momo and also Má Teodora. My mother calls me Má Teodora so I won't forget The Inscription. We all have an inscription. A birth certificate. Civic bonds we cannot throw off.

That is my goal, to throw them off.

I am Momo and I remember that thanks to Cassiopeia I met that man. Gray. Like the others. The one who is almost my father or thinks he is, but does not asked me what I think about that strange paternal love, because if he did I would be struck dumb. And so I get up from the table because I have a lot of plans, pretentious ones, and I do not want to break them for anything in the world.

Making plans is the least we can do. Plan. Plan ourselves.

I am Momo and I knock back the bottle. Hidden among the roses. The bottom of the bottle tastes of Spring dew. Rain in May. Magic elixir.

I am Momo and ring ring, the white telephone with blue numbers rings. Ring ring until my mother looks up and calls me stupid, don't you hear that damned telephone? And I realize yes, I hear it. I have been hearing it since it started ringing and her thick voice called me stupid. Are you not you going to call me again or show any sign of life?

I do not know how to show signs of life. I only know how to give love. All I know is how to drink with you from that bottle and leave when we are done. Hidden among the roses.

I am Momo and my heart is not the same, because it begins to beat irregularly. Real cardiac insufficiency. And I'm scared to stop being Momo the living and begin to be Momo the dead. But I pick up just the same.

Hello?

I am Momo and I act exactly like a daughter is supposed to act. The Momo of the book in my head laughs at me disgustingly.

We will not tell our little secrets. I am telling you how I do it with each gray man I meet in the street. The gray men are like statues.

How do I do it or undo it?

And here comes the wave of advice that I cannot keep in my head because I am stuck, the sound of his voice, his thick melodic voice.

You should ask yourself, Momo. The least we can do is protect ourselves. So I say yes, I will do what you say, and what is it you say.

I am Momo in my bed arranging the books he has given me since we met. Randomly. We both tripped over Cassiopeia at the same time. Like everyone made for one another meet. The worst thing is that Cassiopeia is still alive. I cannot stand her. She's a strange tortoise that only eats entrails.

To be made for each other is the least we can do.

And we must do that well.

The first thing I pick up is a novel written by him and on the first page I read: For my dear fantastic Momo, with lots of love. A novel called *The Interminable Story*.

What love. What a great love.

I am Momo and I decide to call him. Not even the possibility that Michael Ende might love me is able to calm me down. Michael Ende helped mama raise me. With the pretext of helping me pay for Cassiopeia's expenses, he began visiting us almost every day. Then he wrote that book everyone loves so much.

I am Momo and I am alone.

I am Momo and I am abandoned.

The gray men destroyed the city and I do not give a shit. The gray men give me pleasure. I give them pleasure. We exchange pleasure, but I end up winning. I deserve a few free bottles for being stupid. Yes. Stupid.

Hello? Michael Ende? I just want you to know that I only love you. Like in the movies.

I am Momo and I am going on a trip.

If this was a movie there would be a black sign that would say THREE YEARS LATER. Ring ring and my disgusting mother answers, it's for you. And we make a date to go for a beer although my boyfriends will come too. Gray ones. And they surround me with their huge manly biceps (the thing is, I cannot live without them), like in the movies.

To live without others is the least we can do.

And we make up stories about what we will do when we cannot

swallow any more beer.

Why did you go, Momo? Because he never gets drunk with his characters. His characters are afraid of him. And to think I could give him all the love he needs, but he thinks that so much love is for idiots.

Why did you come back, stupid? And now we are completely drunk.

I am Momo and I laugh. I have been running away for three years. I dreamt of something that was never really in my hands. Or in my feet. Something beyond any of my bodily organs. I risked knowing I would fail. But I never abandon a dream without trying it first. Paradoxically, my happiness and satisfaction reside in trying. Later it is the dream that abandons me. I guess I am contradicting myself.

I am Momo and I cry. I cry so much that if this were a Mexican picture I would win the prize for best actress.

I am in control.

I have enough talent to seduce the most handsome man in the world, until my two boyfriends look in and call me stupid, why do you treat us like this. But it is nirvana and I cannot hear anything now, only ring ring in my ear and ring ring beneath my skirt.

Let it rise. Let it open. Let it disappear.

And I know he will save me and take me to his bed. And he will remove the rest of my underwear. Like in the movies. I know he is so drunk he will meow. To meow is the least we can do. And he will not stop in his desire to kiss Momo. His Momo. Who grew. Who got fat. Who stopped time. Who defended the city from the gray men. Who left and came back. By the same road.

Dazra Novak

The Stalker

—It's her!—shouted Alejandro and grabbed the magazines from my hand.

I had enough time, of course I did, that's why I took off running. At the corner of 23 and L she got into a collective taxi with that calm that women sometimes have. The truth is, I thought she would be more agile, maybe because we tend to think of people the way we want them to be. I didn't even think about what I would say to her, I just threw myself in front of the taxi like a crazy man, I ignored the driver's insults and when he asked me where I was going I said: forget about it. Most women would have be been scared, but not her, she seemed to be deep in thought and the truth is I didn't even see that serious face people talk about. She's pretty small, and I admit, that disappointed me, with everything she writes I thought she would be a great big woman, the kind all the black guys turn around and whistle at.

Now that she was so close I thought of each and every scene in *Public Body*. I could imagine her in the stories she tells in that book and see her there, in the flesh, just for me. On top, underneath, naked but for a military cap, with another woman or two, with a guy or two. She took out a black Moleskine and pretended to write something, but just then the woman to her left got out and the three of us had to exit the cab. I took the opportunity to look right at her, measure myself against her. God, she only reached my shoulder. So fragile, so delicate, such a miniature, with her curls falling down her back and her long thin nose. *Bonsai ass*, José Miguel had called her and I thought he was joking, the way writers tend to joke around among themselves. But it wasn't a bad ass, I thought, in any case, after she got in again. Now I was closer to her and until 23 and Paseo I managed to see what she was writing in her Moleskine: *my hand closed the distance too quickly,*

so quickly that she hadn't yet finished urinating. She didn't resist. I felt the
warm urine running across the palm of my hand and dripping down.

Bitch. I'm sure she wrote that on purpose. I turned away on the
seat and she stopped writing and looked out the window again. I
took advantage of the potholes and edged closer and closer to her, so
much so that the driver began looking at me in the rearview mirror. I
remembered the story by Evelyn Pérez: "I Too Spent the Night with
Dazra Novak," and I thought about ending up like the guy in the
story, ending up feeling sorry for her. Maybe she really is a virgin, I
thought and it seemed so possible that I got weak in the knees. She
had let the Moleskine fall on her thigh, and now I could read it better.
She stuck the ballpoint pen between her teeth and I think she was bit-
ing it all the way to 23 and 12. After that she sucked on it knowingly,
that's right, she sucked and sucked on it as if that damned fucking
ballpoint tasted like strawberry, caramel....

I told her. In a burst of courage. I didn't even think twice. I told
her it was me who had been writing to her, because I'd gotten her
mail and couldn't help myself after reading her *Public Body*. She was
deserving of my best poems. I didn't care that she hadn't answered,
not even a line, I wasn't expecting an answer, of course not, she must
get lots of obscene things from people who think she is a... But no,
I don't think that, not me. She made a gesture with her lips like she
didn't believe my story, and she sighed. She looked out the window
and the wind whipped her curls across her forehead. I smelled her hair,
her perfume 212 by Carolina Herrera, just like in her novel *Making
Of.* So it was true!

I told her I admired her a great deal, she had to be very brave to
write like that, without inhibitions. How did she make those things
up? Because it couldn't all be true. Or was it? She looked at me side-
ways, like intelligent women do when they begin to lose patience.
Then she turned back to look outside again, and that's when I saw her
breasts for the first time. The short skirt wasn't the thing, even though
it revealed those tender thighs, their well cared for skin, there's plenty
of thighs in this city. It's a fact. But José Miguel hadn't mentioned
her breasts, he'd only talked about her *bonsai ass*; neither had Evelyn's

story referred to her tits, emerging from her neckline now, round and perhaps a bit too abundant for a body as small as hers. I thought of the story "Cocaine Tea" when she goes down on the guy without even having kissed him on the mouth. I told her I mostly write poems, that I had several books, but none of them were that good and I gave them to a friend who corrected them. I'm very demanding and don't really call myself a writer, that's why I never enter contests, because I take myself very seriously as far as my literature is concerned.

Then in her calm melodic voice, unafraid, she asked me:

So how do you expect others to believe in you if you don't?

That's when we got to the curve just before Almendares Bridge, and out of my nervousness I fell awkwardly away from her. I barely managed to right myself and take her hand to show her that's not what I was thinking, that I'm not the romantic type, given to caresses, bouquets of flowers and Mariachis at the sea wall. She remained calm all the way along 41st Avenue. Too calm. Suspiciously calm. I risked a bit more and braided my fingers in hers, brushed her thigh with the back of my hand and her Delfin skin surprised me with its incredible softness. I ventured one, two, three more motions. Because I couldn't think of anything else, I blurted out:

—Maybe we could have tea one of these days and look at my poems.

And I knew I'd blown it. I watched as she put the Moleskine back in her purse, and I knew I'd blown it. We were coming to Tropicana when she leaned forward and told the driver:

—Here, please.

Before getting in again, I noticed she made the peace sign with her hand, just a couple of seconds, and then continued to the middle of the street. As she waited on the median before crossing the rest of the way I saw that her blouse was pulled up a bit and I could see the tattoo, the sparrow she'd talked about in the book *Reserved Body*, just on her right buttock, on its way to her hip. So it was true....

Cirenaica Moreira

The Power of Universal Attraction and French Fries

...and I close my eyes and dream he's pushing his whole self into me from behind while I'm making black beans. His long hard dick— I dream—black like these black beans, red like the red beans he'll come to eat tomorrow and every day...because he's still dreaming of his cock inside me, more, just a little more. We are in Paris, in the tiny kitchen of his tiny room, where kitchen and bedroom and bathroom and living room and messed up study are all in one. He is at least twenty years older than me, but in my forties you really can't tell the difference. Me at the edge of the table and him. Me at the edge and him. Me without turning around with the knife and the onion in my hands, the bell pepper, the cutting board, his cock between my legs. He still calls to me in the distance. I still conserve the image, stopped in memory, of when he was the one who was twenty years older. Tall, tall, unmistakable, slim and sharp featured, sharp gestures, sharp face, chameleon-like, and his seventies *drum* indelible in my mind, he was worth pointing out, worth choosing, worth having. Now I spot him among many, among the crowd and noise at the *opening*. The plastic cups and red wine. I spot him among the trays, the finger food and historic hunger of a member of the diplomatic corps, badly disguised among all the *mercí* and *mernó*...beneath the recycled, badly ironed, badly cut suits, faded, assigned to each.... I don't know who he is, I don't yet know who he is but I identify him. I don't know who he is but the force of universal attraction envelops us both, it's the force of universal attraction that places his *drum*, that is still his *drum*, in Paris at nine at night on September 27, 2006, standing before me, and above the other heads and berets and barrettes and hairnets and embroideries and blond, black, curly, straight, bald, graying, dyed, dandruff-flaked heads. It is the force of universal attraction placing

us one before the other, above the glasses, the mouths on the rims of the glasses, the laughter, the violins and all the bureaucrats. He looks at me too, he too with his mouth on the glass, his super mouth, and super eyes, looks at me with his chameleon's eyes. Eyes of a chameleon, a viper, a rattle snake, brown eyes of an electric eel, an anaconda... And tall, tall, tall, so tall, so tall, tall... He's been looking at me for a while and now I am running blindfolded through broad hallways, interminable, white, empty, in the old Academy of Fine Arts where he is a student and I am the daughter of the professor and I'm five, six, seven years old and I run in front of him through the whole gallery just because he looks at me. The wet floor, a small puddle on the wood, it could be any puddle made by anything spilled from any of the trays at the *opening*. But it's me, me facing Lamberte who is chasing me from behind, and it's my liquid dripping in the gallery and in his kitchen at Villa Borghese. I ask myself if anyone, in exchange for this small room of his at Villa Borghese and my Havana apartment, would give us any kind of a place in Montmartre. Something big enough for two, in the center of Montmartre or even on the outskirts. I ask myself if in Montmartre or anywhere else, our happiness would be the same.

He still speaks to me from a distance, doesn't stop murmuring lovely words in the distance, beautifully said, about who knows what civilizations and races, as I cleave to his long fingers and black, red, violet cock entering me from behind. From in front, from behind, from in front, from behind. To one side and the other. His long skinny cock like a snake, a Santa María viper. It's not the size or width of his cock that interests me, but the idea of the snake, like a Santa María viper, that I find electrifying. The very idea of him like a snake, like a Santa María viper, its whole length going in and out of me, excites and arouses me. I come to Paris for its black beans and I come with everything, with the bell pepper, the onions, the bay leaf, the knife, the oregano and even the cutting board, the gingham apron and the handkerchief tied around my forehead...a dreamed of paradise that in other circumstances would leave a lot to be desired. I don't need Lamberte to give me anything. I give everything to Lamberte. The dishwasher and clothes washer and vacuum cleaner and mop and lawn mower,

the three-in-one and the DVD and the LCD, the newspaper and stool to rest your feet, the hair dryer, the razor, the disposable diaper, the twins and even the sugar. Good beans always need their quota of sugar. I come to Paris with the quota of sugar I drip into Lamberte's mouth and onto his cock, and I tell him go on try it out. Lamberte. Lamberte has a strange look on his face, he looks at me strangely, and I ask myself if it's Lamberte who is looking at me and not that depraved Henry Miller for whom I have run to Paris a hundred times, a hundred times like he did, without a penny to his name.

Henry Miller hasn't bathed for days, just his cock and ass in the first stall, in case there's a fuck to be had, although I don't think he cares that much, but just in case of a fuck or lice. Nevertheless, beneath his skin, I whiff some cheap cologne that seems too familiar. This man tells me he loves me, that he loves me with abandon, with exultation, and that no woman should ignore a man who loves her like that, that a woman is obliged to repay the love of a man who loves her that way, even if that man is a vagabond and stinks, a sir nobody in the center of Paris, with literary pretensions, an unsuccessful one of a kind pornographer, who roams the streets with a book on his belly, any old book, as if he were a child about to be born, a child men and woman should make way for on the sidewalks, give their seats to on the trolley like they do to children and the elderly. This madman will end up getting me to kneel before him, I know it, he will end up bending me over the stove where one day I will stop making beans, frijoles, lentils, any cheap grain to kill his millennial hunger.

Lamberte makes me kneel and he beats me. I, his trap, his rod, his universal punishment. Where there was a slave, a runaway, now there is once again a man.

Lamberte tells me he loves me as he recites from memory the four hundred forty-one pages of the Cuban edition of Fernando Ortiz's *Deceit of the Races*. A lash for each page, each paragraph, each speech, each deceived Black. I say yes, my lord, whatever you say, my lord, yes, my lord. I beg for forgiveness, I bow, I prostrate myself before you, dear Lamberte, and humbly beg your forgiveness, on behalf of all slave owners and traffickers, on behalf of all the colonizers and

overseers and foremen and captains general and princes and princesses and overseas kings. I should cry about this too, and I do cry. Then Lamberte, transcultural as he is, kneels beside me and prays. Four hundred forty-one Our Fathers. One for every page in the Cuban edition of *Deceit of the Races* by Fernando Ortiz. One for each paragraph, each speech, each deceived Black, for every lash. And we are at peace. Now Lamberte and I run together, hand in hand, beneath the starry blue sky of the classrooms and halls of the old Academy of Fine Arts. I am five, six, seven years old, and Lamberte still wears his white smock. All those years later, at the Paris *opening*, Lamberte remains that identical student, the same white marble dust on his hands, beneath his nails, in his ears, his teeth and hair, the same *drum*, the same familiar odor, although I still can't entirely identify it, or him.

Doubled over the small table as he has me, this Henry Miller fills my ear with his five-foot-eight-inch tongue, so I can't even hear myself think. I should think of Hugo and the money it cost him so I could live in Paris in a house like this one, with two floors and servants like these, and a garden and patio and back patio and flowers that fall from the sky all year round, and a swimming pool and *jacuzzi* and cast iron furniture in the sun, the warm sun of Paris, where I can drink tea and rest my beautiful head and my beautiful little hat and my impeccable black velvet dress, or my dress of ordinary muslin, strawberry-fresh that—Henry says—show off my legs. Henry, oh Henry...everything bought by him, by Hugo, expensive, expensive, so expensive. I should think more about Hugo and about how much he's spent so that I can, still, write in my diary, in my many diaries, each of the dirty words Henry Miller whispers in my ear, slow and clear so I won't get lost in his speech, as well as my own words that are a lot by now and pretty raunchy too, and I still dream of publishing them and scandalizing those who need to be scandalized. Isn't it true that we are predestined, this Henry Miller and me—I manage to ask myself in a trip of his tongue—for some power of attraction? Universal? Cosmic? That makes us useless and serfs at one and the same time? Penitents and serfs? Seduced into helplessness? I should think more about Hugo who brought me to Paris and of his life so I would no

longer be a lonely child, but this Henry Miller also spends a lot on his coarseness. And with his tongue moving through the whole labyrinth of my auditory cavity, he doesn't tire of repeating that monogamy is like being made to eat French fries every day, every single day, as he enters me from behind with everything he has and I see stars, all the stars of Paris's blue sky, of Montmartre, of the Versailles Palace, of the whole French countryside. I close my eyes and the stars are still there. Then I think about the French fries and the grease they're floating in, and in the day to day, and I turn around, I grab his butt and all of him because how I love that pig. Yes, I love this Henry Miller, and the lonely child who also lives in him and in every one of those pages he writes and carries on his belly as if he were a child about to be born. I adore him. I really adore him. I'm telling you. At the same time, I ask myself if, in some way, we haven't tasted the first French fry.

I throw my shoe at the insect on the wall and Lamberte and Hugo and Henry Miller are before me, their cocks just out of the oven and still swollen, and they are looking at me in silence, in the two for one of Havana, Montmartre.... And I set the table with steaming black beans, without sugar or salt. I no longer know who they're for. And I close my eyes....

Havana, January 2013

Margarita Mateo Palmer

Ínclita of Mamporro Speaks

Crazy the two of them. Together. The writer and her friend, who as they look at church documents from the 16th century give free reign to their thoughts and begin to imagine fictions. Crazy, those two women. The two women, I like to say. The author of *El monte* and the female titan of Rojas. Marta Vesa's mother was also delirious as she took part in the game they'd invented: make me flesh, Ínclita of Mamporro, at the train station, so the Spanish philosopher can finally meet her admiring Trinidadians, me, embodying this elegant and proper lady with her red purse, vanity and suitcase, matching her belt and shoes of shiny patent leather, waiting for the train from Las Villas and who smilingly greets, oh yes, with deep affection, is finally able to meet her, María, I have your book *Hacia un saber sobre el alma* so you can sign it for me, it's all underlined, covered with notes, in really bad shape, battered by so many readings, but of great value to me, and more so now that it will bear your signature.

And I, Ínclita de Mamporro, letting myself be carried away by bland small talk when my spirit, meant to try its luck in other regions, would have preferred to take advantage of that unique opportunity some other way, but no, I had no choice but to look at myself in that improvised traveler's get up, her ridiculous train outfit, oh yes, what joy that we met, even so briefly, but I never come to the capital, I hate the noise, I will return to take refuge in my welcoming town, my native land, such a shame that from this rapid meeting all I have is your name in my book. Hopefully we can meet again, with more time, to talk about our common interests, but they're calling my train, oh yes, a kiss, an embrace, delighted to meet you. And I witnessed the end of my time on earth as Lydia and Titina led Zambrano to the car, and I returned to the world of embarrassed fiction, to wait for another

performance that would allow me to insert myself through that brief fissure into the real world. And while the traveler who was me got a rental car to take her home, her enchanted moment shattered, I went back to remembering the words that had illuminated me as if I were living in fiction. Not those words that, dying of laughter, had occurred to the two delirious women of the country house in San José, but the original letters of the missive that might be considered my birth certificate:

Trinidad, October 22, 1951

Dear María:

To express admiration, offer praise, give a compliment, has been a family tradition, cultivated from an early age. That's why, learning of your friendship with Lydia Cabrera, who has been visiting our home for years, I don't hesitate to write to tell you how greatly impressed I am by your book. First it was *Isla de Puerto Rico (Nostalgia and esperanza de un mundo mejor)*, which I read in the La Verónica edition, lent to me by an old school friend. There I found wise ideas about insularity, a subject in which I am passionately interested. Since then I have looked for what you've published, and although I am up to date—I recently read "De la paganización," just out of the oven so to speak—it was my reading, a few years back, of "La metáfora del corazón," in an issue of *Orígenes* that Pogolotti's friends sent me, that confirmed my admiration for your persona and your work. What could I tell you about that marvelous essay that your illustrious friends haven't already mentioned? In any case I don't want to fail to say that in "Las catacumbas," when you speak of the need for going inside oneself to find that tiny but glowing flame that is lit in the depths and illuminates thought, I felt that the idea needed further development. Soon after, my desire was surpassed in your flawless essay.

I do not wish to impose myself. I only wanted you to know that in this old village in the central part of the Island you have a fervent admirer who follows your work with great interest.

Cordially,
Ínclita de Mamporro

The dialogue we sustained from then on, and the breath of life that arrived by post, were intense. In all of it I was able to express my deep admiration for the Malaga native, and simultaneously affirm my precarious existence: in phrases such as "the secret Cuba," or questioning a statement in "Las ruinas," all the time exchanging opinions about the work of our mutual friend, Lydia.

From my diffuse and incorporeal world, from this other dimension where I can only attentively observe how the real world passes by, I anxiously awaited the moment in which I would once again be able to write those letters that gave me life, that caused me to shine in the lace of starry nights, that permitted me to murmur in my interpreters' ears words meant for the great thinker. I have lived in a permanent state of movement, searching for the veins that open to reality. Sweet fiction, enchanted image, Sor Juana's dream that tries to trick the prison built by fantasy. Always waiting for human distractions, always ready to remake myself in them or in their writing. I have waited many years with the hope of a brief return to life. At times, from some Old Havana rooftop, I have tried to discover the green ray of an insular twilight, hoping for the impossible. It has been in vain. With María Zambrano and Lydia Cabrera dead, and the enchantment of my birth broken, only a miracle could revive me.

Irela Casañas

Descent

"I am on my island, safe and sound, everything will be fine,"
I whispered to myself....

—Susan Barton

The plane landed around two in the afternoon and as soon as I emerged I felt a shot of heat and humidity. My skin ignited beneath the intensity of direct sunlight. This caused me to stop for a moment. Finally, I was able to continue on, and it was a good thing because those in the line behind me were impatient and beginning to express their irritation.

It was strange. Both of us had spoken extensively in the letters we'd written, but when we saw one another we had nothing to say. We each knew who the other was. What we liked, even what we didn't. Time flew and suddenly we didn't know what to do with it. We were somewhat awkward, and after a mutual effort relaxed and tried to make plans. I had a lot and he very few. He told me he was repairing his house, an old one. He made translations from the English but didn't have many clients because where he lived there weren't many people who needed that service. He spent his afternoons fishing, just for fun, and continued to be a music lover like me. Just before saying goodbye, I gave him a small package. Records, I told him. He thanked me. He didn't open the package. We hugged each other, close like I no longer imagined possible, just like in our letters.

Seventeen years have passed. I am with him now. I live in his house. He's one of those who rent rooms to tourists in this small village with a view of the Atlantic. I guess I should write wonderful things about this place, its people, its climate.... I'm a bit tired. I am forgetting how to maintain my distance. This society isn't as

simple as those from elsewhere think. I am getting soft. I've become involved with my oldest lover but I'm interested in equilibrium. Neither is he as simple as he seemed. He is more attached to the ordinary passage of the days than to our dialog. At night, he is warm and outgoing.

He never had children and doesn't want them. He says he always thought he would one day give his time to another, but never felt like he was ready. Now he thinks he has too much time. Some guests arrive, they stay for three days, they leave, then others come. Some of them are friendly, others aren't. He tries to make everything go all right. He prefers to keep his papers up to date. He has time to read, listen to music, do exercises, above all swim. You're still young, I tell him. He tries to smile and succeeds. Look at your skin. And your well-proportioned profile. You have a sensual chest. I tell him all this but he thinks I'm kidding, that he doesn't deserve it.

In the afternoons, during all-out summer as he called the months from May to September, around seven at night he'd sit on the terrace and drink a cocktail while he watched the sea. He doesn't know how to measure his drinks and would always serve himself another. Sometimes I'd approach him little by little and depending on what the profile of his lips would tell me, I'd stay at his side or leave. Because I don't like people talking to me or touching me when my mind is far away, I am very careful during his most intimate moments. These days they are talking about the fact that in several parts of the island they are making people leave who live close to the sea, so they can extend tourism. He doesn't talk about it but I can tell he's afraid. He forebears have lived in this house since the 19th century. They resisted everything, from the wars of independence to the depression in the thirties. From the 1959 Revolution to the crisis in the nineties. Against his will at the beginning, he has conserved this beautiful colonial house. He has worked hard fighting the residue of salt, hurricane-strength winds and the bad taste of insolent construction workers. Now he is afraid. I don't think the village will be transformed so suddenly. But he knows the country better than I do. I abandoned it when I was still a child, when change still excited me.

I know these days will come to an end. I must return to London with my article done and wanting to write and continue discovering little-known places that tourists would like. A few days ago, precisely in the morning, after going out to buy vegetables, I said we needed to talk. Immediately he took my hands and led me out into the street again. I didn't expect that reaction; the street wasn't the best place to talk. Nevertheless, we walked to a small set of steps. Will you climb with me? Of course, I said. Slowly, and with the sun beating down, we climbed those tiled steps that led to a small plaza where two metal umbrellas challenged the wind and there was a little stand where they sold beer. From a radio, you could hear a fast and danceable rhythm, but the four or five men who were there seemed lost in thought. They sat there with their arms outstretched toward their mugs and their gazes vague. Only one, who may have been in his thirties, seemed to be talking to himself under one of the umbrellas. From there, you had a magnificent view of the village and of the coast. As if time hadn't passed. Only a wind park far to the left spoke of the century in which we lived. The fishermen's boats rested here and there close to shore. Their owners had worked until dawn. I don't know why, but at that moment I remembered a passage in a Kawabata novel in which the writer describes the bustle of a beach community. And I laughed at my ignorance of those years in which one supposed the Japanese incapable of raising a ruckus. Then I laughed at myself again because for a long time I couldn't imagine Cubans capable of silence.

In the end I will say yes. And I will rescue him from that complacent immobility. As for me, I've learned to feel good. I know how to bear up in the heat and humidity. I walk the streets and I'm not irritated when people stare at me. Three times a week I run, always along the coast. Then I shower. I leave my sweater and shoes in the sand. I feel very relaxed. Once in a while someone has robbed me, and I've been forced to walk home in my bikini. And so I've had to simulate peace. One of those times someone yelled: *but that's the limit, who does she think she is?* I don't understand them completely. They are incredibly relaxed but in some cases pretty conservative. They don't protest

around important issues but never fail to express trivial concerns. If someone wears something or fixes her hair differently from the majority, there's always someone who dares to express his inconformity and make a joke in really poor taste. There are women who still aren't able to postpone motherhood or have a few beers with their friends. Nevertheless, groups of men do so all the time.

Many people ask me what I do here. Why so long, when tourists mostly come for three days? I don't feel like a tourist, but I don't feel Cuban either. I feel a little bit English, but that doesn't make much difference. I want to find a root that is stronger than nationality.

Some nights, if there are no guests, we put on the music we say is from our time. And here, in this creole atmosphere, we might listen to Cinderella, Motley Crue, REM or Iron Maiden...all depending on his mood. Then we talk as if we had lived that time together.

We are emotionally similar. The differences emerge when he asks me to tell him in detail about the big band concerts. Then I open up, and he goes mute. I was at a concert where Motley Crue's drummer played a whole set above the audience. It was hallucinatory. Maiden is spectacular on stage. When I was twenty-two I took a photograph of myself with Bruce Dickinson. I think I sent it to him.

It is October and the sky dawned gray. A light rain. Some people walk by the house saying: "What an ugly start to the day." The facades of the old houses, the street and trees are all in shadow. They say a cyclone is coming. The sea has lost its usual splendor. My mood also begins to give way. I'm changing a little. I long for a day of blinding light. I am becoming a small-town woman who's forgotten how to drive fast and is so accustomed to the smell of the sea that she doesn't even notice it.

It's commonplace to see men with their foreheads furrowed because their soccer team lost. When this happens, there are those who badmouth the athletes. But when they win I know they would allow themselves to be kicked by their idols. Not my man. My man is so serene and carries such personal pain that he doesn't express it even in gestures. I want to give him the chance to repeat his youth.

Although I sometimes want to withdraw, how can I help a man increase his vitality?

You know I want you to come with me? He is afraid. Above all, he is afraid that something he has so fervently desired won't be as he imagined. We can travel, go to concerts. We can return anytime you want.

Both of us know very well there is no reason to return.

Charo Guerra

Other Memories of J.B.

Dear Soleida,

For *El retrato ovalado* I prefer to give you this letter (unpublished to now) by Yvone de Uhrbach,[3] woman of Cuban origin who lived—and ended her days well into the 20th century—giving classes at an art school in Mexico. Its contents seem to indicate that it may well be one of the last messages sent by Juana Borrero Pierra to Carlos Pío Uhrbach Campuzano. If this can be corroborated, we are looking at a hopeful (and less tragic) version of both their final days,[4] although the official version insists they died: she of typhoid fever at the age of eighteen (March 9, 1896 in Cayo Hueso) and he of starvation the following year (December 17 or 24, at a rebel camp in Colón). He was twenty-five. Although some scholars believe that the testimony I transcribe here is apocryphal, her executor, Estela Owens,[5] holds documents and articles that can legitimize the provenance of the original manuscript: a poem titled

3 Remember that Yvone was the pseudonym preferred by Juana in her correspondence with Carlos Pío.

4 Or Juana's final days at least. The surname Uhrbach, part of what we imagine is a pseudonym, also makes us consider a possible meeting with Carlos, although it might also have been a desired choice in her new identity. I refer here to a comment made by Carlos in a letter sent to his brother Federico, on August 10, 1896: "I tell you that I will end up believing her alive and live deceived by that illusion" (quoted in Belkis Cuza Malé, *El clavel y la rosa. Biografía de Juana Borrero*, Ediciones Cultura Hispánica, Instituto de Cooperación Iberoamericana, Madrid, 1984. p. 219).

5 Linked with Casal through family on her mother's side. Her wish (she has told me) is to generously gift them to a Cuban institution that will authenticate and keep them safe.

"No" (in which Borrero's voice and writing can be found) and an oil painting (signed JB), the details of which match the description Julián de Casal made of a landscape painted by her,[6] to date undiscovered by Cuban art critics.

A hug,
Charo

February 11, 1896:

It's nighttime and everyone in the house sleeps. No one notices the pallid light by which I write these lines. My fountain pen races across the paper, I want to get this torrent of ideas out; they will continue to torture me if I do not share them with you, if I do not stop being a hypocrite and find the courage to clarify some of those intimate contradictions that we humans tend to hide behind panic. What I've always promised in my letters, Carlos, but never end up doing: allow you to see my soul.

From the moment we are born, some people begin to look for a coherent profile, a phrase that matches our spirit, an idea to hold onto. And then we consciously cooperate with that idea, we create our best and most popular image; we live enslaved to it. Pure manipulation, pure deception, vulgar pretension; I, who include myself in that group, want to be able to break it all open.... And I feel myself new, distinct, a different person since I try to dissolve the constraints that have guided my life to this point. Authentic, yes that word fits now. Why must I forever be the helpless *sad virgin*; why accept a symbol (pathetic, not poetic) that only announces fatality. What sort of a compliment is

6 Reading the passage, we can take as exact these words that Casal published in his chronicle "Juana Borrero" (*La Habana Elegante*, July 15, 1892):
... a lonely door of cracked wood and oxidized hinges, in the middle of a broad wall, mottled with the green and black of humidity and decked out in flowers. In front of the wall, there is a winding pathway sewn with pebbles that sparkle in the sun. Stalks of wild plants grow here and there. To the left is a river with grassy shores, like a silvery silk ribbon about the waist of a tunic of green velvet.

Julián's bad omen; I loved him only because of his rejection, in order to immerse myself in pain (as if he had understood that he would be the Apollo of my poem, since when writing it, without even knowing him, I foreshadowed such fantasy...). Why struggle to prove his ill-fated certainties? I accept the fact that the confusion of his ("Sad virgin") meant prestige and recognition for me, social notoriety, attention from others; but now, hearing them so often, I detest those lines. I would like to erase them from my history, disassociate them from my name. And as I know this isn't possible, at this point all that is left is for me to change my life. (These fevers have helped me arrive at drastic decisions.... More sure than ever, I want to work: I will give painting lessons in the classic style of my friend and teacher, Menocal, but I will teach by creating, I will demand opinions, my students' critical participation.) I want to belong to the century to come.

February 15:

Over the past few days I've barely managed to sleep and, when I am able to doze my mother appears again with nausea-inducing syrups. They have bled me, my body is broken from so many violations, tortures I can no longer endure. My palette and my body demand other balms: to taste fruits fallen from the trees, to bite into them, my own hands cutting them like ordinary people do, walking, running, shouting. I am an ordinary person. That behavior of freedom, almost savage, would be the proof of my cure; add the medicine of beer... Even my father agreed and yesterday brought me half a dozen.

Today, as at other times, there is a salamander behind the dressing table, it has become my confidant these days; it appears and disappears and assumes absurd dimensions, and I myself am unsure whether I have imagined that it exists or if it is part of my new vigil-like consciousness. I am going to paint it as soon as I can pick up my brushes again. I have also seen a flower that might be your soul, I have felt the presence of that flower growing in this room where death roams; death wanting at all costs to overpower me and I shouting at it

to get out, it's not yet time. Obedient, she leaves but then returns with her victim's face, death and I have achieved a vicious circle, a dependent and pernicious relationship; I know I will be the winner, I think she finally understands. I explained the scandals that would come and death has given in, she likes brawls, irreverence, knows how to negotiate this wily Ikú; if Tinita's stories are true, the character Death will have to refrain the impulses of her slave Disease, and both will have to distance themselves from me for a long time, if not forever. My God, immortality would be horrible.

Sometimes the salamander and the flower grow so large they no longer fit in this space, suddenly I am a mere insect perching, one more among those who flit about and enjoy its essence, caressing and pampering it as if it were the most beautiful in the garden. On those walks I take as if I were a leech on the stalk, I admire the details of its consistent juicy green texture; I believe I am watched by the sly salamander, I would be able to open my eyes at its slightest false moment, and its clumsy green would devour me. I accept the coexistence of my new partners; yet I can tell you, I am suspicious of everything, of everyone, even of these mad ideas I am spewing and that take me from what I must tell you urgently...

February 17:

This is a message for you, Carlos. I feel it is a sincere conversation, heartbreaking if you want to call it that. You are free to interpret, judge, speak. I will not defend myself with you. I want you to know how for so many years I have swallowed the flame of my passions...yes, passions in plural. Filled with fears because they constitute an unnamable torment, their features undefined, although from childhood on I would find them in the noble expression of a friend or one of my father's colleagues, all of them sitting around the living room praising the genius-child without understanding they were treating her like an adult, loving her as if she were a woman, I even wanted to caress some of them, pretend to be a loving wife, and as a result of those excesses,

I act peculiarly. They prefer to say (and I let them think it) that I am strange. I have lived with the shame of that impudence, trying to make it seem innocent, Esteban's daughter's eccentricity. Later there was Julián, your brother Federico, you, Cay, and others...Only Luciano knows and has been able to understand the fire in my eyes. When my mother, at Tinita's suggestion, wanted us to go to the Spiritual House, she was trying her last resort. She took me behind my father's back because he would not have approved of that decision, not even as a treatment for the paleness the doctors chalk up to rheumatism, Puentes' erratic winds, tropical epidemics.... My mother left, offended. "Insolent mulato, horrifying sick lowlife," she would say. Esteban mustn't find out, this is quackery, belief in the uncouth, I don't know how I let myself be taken in. Don't listen to those things, daughter, don't stain your innocence, what shame, what a mistake, that Luciano is possessed...." How exaggerated were my mother's comments, I see that so clearly for the first time.

He suggested a "ritual" to deal with the demands death was making upon my spirit and body. I had to do a cleansing with corojo oil, coconuts, animals, blood, varieties of honey, prepare a lavish meal: goats, chickens, pigs, hens; the sacrifice would conclude with me ripping my clothing. My mother said "Oh, no, no. No." I immediately understood it was exactly what my body required. And we couldn't have imagined how that ceremony would end, but I could imagine it—at only twelve I could see the scene Luciano and I would carry out: a diabolical dance, and shocking.... The most sincere description is carnal lust. Why should I deny it? He spoke looking straight into my eyes, with words that were badly pronounced, his voice all choked up, he said: "Someone must take her before she is nineteen, save her, she needs a man, the protection of Orula," he shook with emotion.... Like him, I thought, bronze, sweet and determined. To take her, what a delicate way of expressing that which I alone claim, as I listen to each of my body's deep desires.

Papa, confusing politics with things of the soul, so removed from what causes his daughter to languish, thinking the syrups would work miracles. So worried by the misunderstandings between us. He

has told my mother that he fears for me, for the passions that might weaken me, wither me, he said, how much more he would suffer if he knew they were carnal passions. More problems. After Sara de los Angeles' death, my father has turned taciturn. I don't know if he could bear these confessions.

February 20:

When I imagine how the offering with Luciano ends, it is he who attracts me, or it is Julián, or it is you (we must interpret the dream of the growing flower, the salamander's crafty ways). Or it is Josema, the administrator of my father's business, so delicate and strong, always looking at me out of the corner of his eye, thinking I don't notice how the blood rises in his cheeks when he sees me, and then I decide to ask him something, something innocent, trifles a young woman chooses when wishing to select the best words, the best gestures, so she may impress her interlocutor.

I dream, Carlos, forgive me these confessions, a body sometimes emerges out of a daguerreotype, it becomes human so it may possess me, it embraces me from behind and I slowly turn around, without fear, because although I cannot yet see the man's face I know who he is, I have always known him, and I believe in him, I await him fervently. My body tries to alleviate those weaknesses in poetry, but there is nothing more passionate. I try to erase the drawing that is measured and devoid of any bodily reference, yet you yourself bring me those delights ever since *Gemelas*. Poetry ignites my body. Do you know? You know..., It may be your subconscious but there is a lot of fire in those sonnets, there is a Carlos Pío who is very close to me and unknown to others.

February 25:

I don't dare write about any of this, not even in my diary. Each night in my room I await that presence. I feel it arrive and open the bedroom door, move forward but resist approaching me. One of these

nights I left the doors slightly ajar and waited to see if it would come. I drowned in that space, anxious and alone. And then Josema arrived and I took him into my bed, filled with desire. We were on the point of embracing one another but I was frightened by my sister Helena's nightmares and I pushed him gently to the door. Since then, each day under any pretext we have looked for each other, and he has returned to my room. My father, who had begun to suspect something, saw us kissing one another at dawn, bidding each other farewell. I've told him, I write, I tell, you, my other half. (I ask myself if I will really send this letter I never seem to finish, if I will be brave enough…I wouldn't want to provoke the slightest suffering in you).

Following the incident, there were more problems in my family. My health continued to deteriorate, it seemed like rheumatism; perhaps I am being punished for not having listened to Luciano. Tinita reproaches my mother: "Consuelo, destiny is set, if you don't go to it, it will come to you." And to prove her point, she brings up the horror that occurred before our eyes a few months back,[7] says it was a sign, "another warning meant for Juana." Tinita blames destiny, at least it absolves Josema and me of sin, on top of everything, she believes I am saved because I am not yet nineteen. She is very naïve. My mother reproaches herself. She has admitted that we must accompany Luciano all the way, be willing to risk ourselves, put my life in his hands. That if she had been there Luciano wouldn't have overstepped, that I have lived influenced by that prophecy and that's why Josema took advantage (or misinterpreted) my erroneous act of survival, and so forth…. Other naivetés. I explained, directly as is necessary in such circumstances, that for days Josema and I had repressed our will and desire of *grosero cuerpo*…. If I hadn't spoken up in time and with such

7 In his introductory essay to Juana Borrero's *Epistolario*, Cintio Vitier tells stories that can be taken as somber premonitions: …*strange stories such as that knife that vibrated half an inch from her throat and of that dagger Casal gave her, according to what they said, one day when he saw that she was sad; and suddenly as if in brutal response to his obsessions, before his very eyes, the crime was consummated and Radamés, the beloved Black manservant, stabbed Tomasa to death and shot himself.* (*Juan Borrero. Epistolario*, Academia de Ciencias de Cuba, Instituto de Literatura y Lingüística. T. I, Havana, 1966. p. 13.)

force, my father would have killed him. I have accepted my father's forgiveness as an act of love, although his lack of understanding disgusts me (he has aged rapidly of late), it seems as if, by some act of magic, the girl-genius has suddenly become an abject object, dirty, unpresentable, a monster.... And, furthermore, he suffers the betrayal of the man who until now was his unconditional colleague. If everyone knew, I would have to face yet another accusation of witchery, and for a second time I would not be able to bear it.

February 28:

In the end, when they consider my suicide attempts in the light of this episode they will see a connection.... The lesser of all evils. I still love you despite those freedoms. My parents have suffered, but the matter has been managed with absolute discretion. Tomorrow we are going to Mexico (Josema and I); on the way, we will decide the future destiny of our lives. My father believes that death (anticipated, and in so many ways predicted), although it would cause a great deal of pain in the family would be preferable to the alternative of watching me succumb to my sins, the scandal of such a relationship in ethical terms, and where other unfounded histories would emerge, with Julián, with my cousin (you yourself were delirious in your jealousy of him), the broken commitment to you, Carlos, for a reason such as this one, that my father does not hesitate to consider "degrading." Despite the fact that he does not completely accept you, he agrees with your political ideas, he thinks you are about to go to war, which to him denotes not only intelligence but courage...and, all the while, your beloved giving herself to another man, "any other man," he has said (mentioning Josema's racial mix, he could have no other argument because he knows his integrity all too well). Josema, rather than confront him, lowered his head out of respect, no offense matters beside the possibility of joining his life to mine. Above all, he continues to adore doctor Esteban.

March 5, 1896 (in Mexico):

I hope God will bless us, and that this whole confusion ends once and for all. I don't know that physical death would not be more dignified than this decision to separate you and me, my Carlos, and force me—with another identity—to share my life with an honorable, loving man who attends ardently to my flirtations and desires but with whom, if I could freely choose my destiny would be nothing more than a happy adventure. This is not the plenitude to which I aspire, the union that together you and I imagined and in which you must continue to believe despite everything; I fear I will never again find peace, faced with your permanent absence, even in a letter. Even there, in your letters, reading them, feeling your words, your reproaches, I would resign myself, would be happy. I do not want you to go to war. If you go I lose all hope. Please, do not commit such a crazy act as allowing yourself to die believing we will never again see one another. I will put away these notes and keep a copy to remind myself how I have conversed with you. When I establish myself in this city I will send you a way of finding me.

March 9:

I die today in Cayo Hueso. I imagine the impact of this news, on my family and especially on you. I am alive and I love you. It is strange knowing I will never again be called Juana, that I have been reborn with another name and story.

March 20:

The days pass and mysteriously my spirit begins to recover; I no longer have those nightmare-dreams that seemed so real they left me limp, color has returned to my cheeks in Renoir tones. Josema makes sure I am well, he takes good care of me; it may seem a dark sensation but I feel our love in him.

March 21:

How I would love to know that you have been able to achieve your political passions, that you have time to spend with your people, in Matanzas, writing poems, a time of warm rupture I already mourn profoundly. Passionate romantic lines (decadent, didn't our Franz used to say in *Gris y Azul?*), in which it was possible to find hope in definitive return, before another eclipse of the moon, without resentments, grief, or questions about good and evil. I want to know that you live, lover. Mine. Pure in your sentiments, unburdened by the absurd ostentations and social conventions that we have suffered and that I have definitively renounced.

> That is how I love you and
> feel myself still yours,
> Yvone

Note: The margins of this text are covered with flowers drawn in pencil.

Georgina Herrera

Absolved, Madam Mariana

At last.

Independence of body and thought was the code established between you and your people but, despite that code, despite its clarity, you were subjected to a sad, strange and ugly trial.

What might your guilt have been, from that time at the beginning of the wars to this other time, so seemingly different?

What difficult and sordid legacy comes and goes in thought?

But I am here, Madam, standing beside your history like the guard dog that most protects and loves it, and you come to me in the memory of conversations heard in my childhood. Stories preserved in that language one speaks, one hears and remembers, but also intended for an eternal future. Now we understand those intentions, those ways of speaking, pretending praise, unearthing tremendous grace in tremendously dramatic moments. And from such a long time ago, from your only life, unequaled and impossible to equal until mine, I am the one you have designated as your defense. An unnecessary defense if I did not exist to say what I have already said. The ugliness that accommodates itself in thought. You were not understood. There were many who did not want to understand you. But now you take my hands and lift them against your heart. I can feel them. How many unhealed wounds, each multiplying itself in so many bleeding sons and daughters, far from your strange way of loving, but...what love of the whole world in your ways.

No, I do not digress, Madam, I suffer and tremble from so much accumulated fury, from so much time passed. "Mariana threw women crying for their wounded sons from her house, she told them: 'Get out, I want no tears'." One only needed a small amount of superficiality to believe that you were that hard, ungrateful even. Yes, as we

consider them let us call things by their names. Neighbors crying for your numerous sons that left, one by one, without hesitating, always baring their breasts to the enemy's gunfire and you pushing them out. But those neighbors weren't the Only Mother of so many courageous children, some of them falling far from her blessing, others immersed in fever and wounds at the nearby camp. There, there, my Lady, of course you alone could not cry. The cry of such a mother becomes interminable water, and there in waiting were the streams ready for your tears to swell and become mighty rivers.

How, then, could the miracle of the Invasion have taken place? Would the rebels have been able to vanquish every obstacle from one end of the Island to the other, but not the immense ocean of your tears? If you had cried with all your energy and reason, the war would have ended once and for all, Madam. If it continues today, if the water little by little adjusts its level, it is because of you, Madam, because of how your husband died in battle "complying with your wishes," as he said in his agony. What other wife of that time had such fabulous privilege? And your eleven sons, going to their deaths and into exile, separated from their mother's love by the greater love that you yourself taught them!

There, there, Madam Mariana, there. No, I am not so insolent, not so bold as to ask that heart of yours to calm itself, that heart that still beats and bleeds. Such a demand would be impossible. But they were slighting you (and you know it, or you always knew it and did not fight for that, because those who are just never fight for what they know is theirs, but rather wait, as you have, until they have no alternative but to give you your due). You alone have won that great battle, you who stood accused by false praise, by that bourgeois crime of containing all tears in two fists and swallowing them without spilling a drop. Today they finally name you Mother of all Cubans. But leave it to me, for you put my hands on your heart and I remember the stories told all wrong, soon you will be the Mother of the Nation to *all* Cubans. Now the Nation is of mixed blood, an island, cured by suns, races, winds and waters that arrive and stay,

and that is how we claim her. May you have a bit of peace now that I am your war. I am the guard dog that most loves and cares for you.

August 18, 2012

Adelaida de Juan

The Painting

For some time, I have felt the urgent need to portray a scene. It would have been at one and the same time ancient and familiar, a scene that leads to the present. It would show a woman whose features and body were a bit tired, sitting before a sewing machine, and who receives an unexpected messenger.

The bearer of the message is a terribly ferocious being. Even his winged members are painted in black. His face a grimace, he puts his claw on the frightened woman's shoulder....

The inanimate object, the Singer sewing machine, is the only element with a few touches of soft color. Because that's how Giotto painted his skies.

She would follow the painters of the admirable Florentine artist's era and those of previous decades, when they included contemporary people and elements in their vision of biblical landscapes.

The Virgin, young and beautiful in her vestments of many-hued blues, her hands joined in a prayer of gratitude and her face peaceful and illuminated as she receives the good news, standing in a setting such as the one the painter would have known....but transmuting into the twentieth century.

She would paint the woman surrounded by familiar objects, her foot on the pedal of the sewing machine.

The Angel who, with lily and dove has just brought the news, has been transformed into that terrifying being before whose menacing claw the woman seated at the Singer tries to retreat in fear.

Because that news doesn't always come at the best time, it is not always desired, and we do not know if it will finally bring with it a being of unusual strength.

Is that why, without thinking, unconsciously, the hand that guides the brushes will recall something of its own mother?

Antonia Eiriz mixes her colors and begins to paint *The Annunciation*.

Soleida Ríos

The Sentence / Ayón Catalog

1984
Interior of Ñáñigo man / Print, 255 x 185 mm
Masai Woman
Prepared for a clitorectomy / Xilograph, print (etching)
and dry point

1985
Sikán / Colored lithograph
Untitled [Figure with walking stick, pitcher and fish]
Masai myth
Ceremony for initiates and obones
Untitled [Figure laying down, and four on their knees]

1986
Nasakó initiated
Veneration
Oh Tánze!
Syncretism / Tempera on cardboard
...most ancient sacred memory...
They worshipped the green corn stalk
Ekwé will be mine!!!
Nasako keeps watch night and day
Ndísime
Tánze
Untitled [Painted legs and pitcher with fish]

1987

Be careful, woman
Sikán be careful!
Untitled [Double man with spots]
Be careful, Sikaneka!
Stay!
Don't go!!! / Colored lithograph, 224 x 180 mm
Goodbye
Stay!
Come!
Don't go!!! / Colored lithograph, 441 x 180 mm
Oh, Tánze!
Akanabionké, Akaramina, Sikaneka-Sikán
Initiation / Print, 995 x 485 mm

Casuarinas. I love the sound of the wind in the casuarinas. I love...I am afraid of the Poet of Alamar. He is strong, he is... "The Chosen One." There is something that connects us, something powerful I still don't understand. Suddenly, in the middle of the conversation he looks at Cultelli as if he didn't know her and says: Tell me, Marina, are you finally going to take your feet out of the water or not? He doesn't embrace Marina, he embraces S., he embraces the Paraguayan.... But S. and the Paraguayan *are* Marina. Nevertheless, she has complained, she complains:

—S. never had her feet in the water. That damned Paraguayan doesn't have her feet in the water and, furthermore, those drums! She put State Security on my trail with those dollars she gave me when they suddenly sent me to Moscow.... He left, right away, in zig zag, tall, strong, alone, along the Avenue of the Palms. To the Sea. A-la-mar.

But earlier, I was attentive. Between laughter and laughter (not the rattlesnake laugh that the other Angel says I have, but that choking Beckett-like laugh) he belts out a speech one must hear. Portentous voice that rises and falls like the sound of the wind in the casuarinas. And we had to listen to him:

—Marina Abramović…, you got naked, you removed your skin, just for once, naked, you came onto the stage. You and your photo in the background, on the wall, And above, the Solitary Star. Ten years now. Ten years. Just once. You radiated. You-went-wild. A whole bottle of honey, a whole bottle of wine, swallow after swallow, utterly calm, in the little crystal glass. You squeezed it, you broke the glass, you bled, you, Marina Abramović. And the razor blade traced another star. Five bleeding points from/on your body. Later, the whip in your right hand, flaying yourself, skinning your back, your back like a face before the audience, and you, your face gazing at your own reflection splattered on the wall, in back. Blood blood blood, Marina Abramović…

Body resting, in the shape of a cross. A cross of ice. Quiet, Marina (go on and take those damned feet out of the water!!!). Cold beneath your body Abramović and, from the ceiling, a ray of heat, burning, inciting, settling the score, pushing the blood blood blood blood….

And Marina quiet, laid out in the form of the cross, relaxed. Abramović body quiet, bleeding out.

Ex-pressing herself. Pig Gallery! What is it that Marina Abramović wants…?

The insolent unbearable public will raise you up.

Look at my hands, look at me, bleeding, in this bathtub.

Sikán, mother of the spirits, great being of the sea from which we come and to which we will return
Adoration
 To be adored…

1988
The dinner / Print, 1379 x 3000 mm
 …they adopt expressions of surprise, pessimism, grief,
 indifference, curiosity before the act that has been
 committed…
The lord of the secret

Sikán
Ndisime
Initiation II
Fishing I

 ...fishing, and the leopard man provocatively displaying his desires...

Fishing II

 ...consummation of the event [...] the loss [...] displaced by patriarchy's triumph.

1989

Abasí, save us
Sikán
Sacrifice
They sacrificed and venerated her

1990

Sikán [Crucified]
Although we go to heaven they will always remember us

1991

Now we are here
So that you will always love me / Print, 4367 x 2100 mm
The family

 ...Gauguin's work Ana the Javanese *[...] that marked me [...]that figure so quietly seated.*

The consecration / Print, 2300 x 3030 mm
The dinner
Mokongo

 Shepherd-king [...] determined, sure of himself, on his divine throne, his itón, staff of supreme justice....

Nlloro
Untitled [Sikán with walking stick]

1993

Untitled [Sikán, Nasakó and Holy Spirit]
> *He tries to reconcile himself with men and wants them to pardon him.*

Our duty
> *They sacrifice her again.*

I gave you to power
> *...she gives her power to men.*

The sentence / Print, 960 x 670 mm
> *...constantly threatened by two serpents, wounded by sharp branches...*

Untitled [Man with Sikán in his hands]

Has she repented?
> *...tearing at her skin in a sign of ambivalence...*

I always return
> *It always returns, history repeats and reaffirms itself with* Pa' you who will always love me.

The procession
Where are you?
> *Men look for something, the secret.*

Untitled [Sikan with a goat]
> *...two beings who will always share a single destiny, sacrifice.*

Limbo
Vendicta
Untitled [Sikán with black dots]
Untitled [Sikán with white dots]
> *Death, retelling of the myth.*

My soul and I love you
Untitled [Sikán entering the river]
Untitled [Sikán with serpents and a white cross]
> *Man's threat and powers.*

Let us go
> *Sikán's resurrection among the women with the secret.*

1995

Mbori (box)
Sleeping
Untitled [White figure kneeling in the center]

1996

Untitled [Figure floating in a sea of fish scales with labyrinth]
 Sikán is levitating [...] it is she, her body, her soul,
 the two of them, they are *united at the spine,*
 but separated by the labyrinth of loss...
Untitled [White figure below covering her face, labyrinth of borders]
...of woman's sacrifice [...] where there is always an executioner
Untitled [woman in fetal position]
Untitled [Black figure carrying a white one]
Untitled [Women disrobing]
Untitled [White torso with black hand on its face]
Untitled [The noose and the fire]
 ...the intense expression in her eyes blames or invites us
 to dream about her suffering: will it be the noose, will
 subjecting ourselves to anything be our salvation?
 Our hands and feet are almost completely bound but
 there is always some escape, some solution, a light...

1997

Giving and giving
Tribute...
Unfounded fears
Let me go!!

 Corner of 12th and 19th, Vedado. Valentine's Day.
 ...They said he asked for rice and beans, she says, macho banana, ripe, fried, quimbombó...and didn't taste a bite.
 He jumped, they said. It was a low window, it sucked him out. The Poet exploded his black head, below, against

the wall: Nothing? No One? A

Number?, The Foreigner? The Other? Zero at Birth? The Ox?, The Damaged Orphan? Escobar.

At the very same time in the afternoon, far away (the falcon cried), someone

(mentioned Haydée Santamaría, Artaud, Libertad de Arriba...) predicted

"it is irreversible now."

1998

Intolerance

Harassment

We must be patient / Print, 650 x 650 mm

My vernicle or the wounded slingshot

> *...Fleeting and passionate moment* [...] *hesitant Colombian hat* [...] *face, mask, rag, background.*

My vernicle and if I do not forget you

> *...attachment, fiery missing...*

My vernicle or I only know I love you

> *...fear, adoration, fright...*

My vernicle or your love condemns me

There is always something that escapes us or is inevitable

Perfidy / Print, 2018 x 2520 mm

Fan [*...of two seas*]

Disobedience

Resurrection

Desire

1999

Tranquility?

Untitled [Unfinished] Offset Lithograph, 2080 x 1100 mm

September 11
It is time!!! Now..., the Least, the Sure. The Instant. I love the metals, I love the speed, I love the laughter. The laughter will shake me loose, this convulsive laughter will take me to the Place

August 24, 2012

Homage to B.A. All the quotes are from *Nkame. Well thought out catalog by Belkis Ayón* (Havana, 1967-1999), Madrid, Editorial Turner, 2010.

Adriana Normand

Arts Theater

Rather than maintain predetermined states of mind, I wanted to see beyond them.

My mother and my grandmother, her mother and grandmother, and all the mothers and grandmothers before them repeatedly warned that it is best not to play with certain things.

I want to play and I play, but my body bears the evidence of my crime.

—You will become so accustomed to blood it will no longer frighten you, but don't lose your respect for it, don't let it touch your hands more than necessary, don't allow its strength to control you.

My grandmother, for example, abandoned her only left leg at the hospital.

The first man who took it and separated it definitively from her body wore a mask and gloves like a scrupulous assassin.

The cut was deep, clean, pitiless.

A clean cut, is the phrase, and it was.

We sink our steel blade in the skin and flesh that is still good, we turn the healthy part rotten as well.

I didn't say company, but inheritance.

I couldn't do it then except from loneliness, there was something very theatrical in my gesture, but all else was simply an audience composed of the blind and the mute.

As in the old myths I have become one with the world and, even so, I haven't stopped being defined by my race.

I have melted into the background and allowed that image to transcend me.

I wanted to drag myself, sink myself, hide myself, find a center, and at times I came close to getting there.

It is not true that my gods, all my gods, abandoned me, I only had to call their names, they were living inside me like inhabitants of an ancestral cave.

I have disobeyed the warning and penetrated the space where there is no hope.

What I found didn't make me stronger or wiser, but more real.

Since somehow someone will do it, I prefer to sink my metal into my body myself.

And I do so, and it is beautiful.

And I do so again, and they applaud.

I cut my legs, my arms, my face so many times...that I rise above pain and my body becomes weightless.

Four...

Three...

Two...

One...

In a single motion I retrieve flesh, blood, and inhabit dust once more.

Dedicated to Ana Mendieta
(Havana 1948 – New York 1985)

Gina Picart

From Another Skin

Ever since I began writing my novel about Hypatia of Alexandria, her correspondence with her favorite student, the Libanese Sinesio of Sirene, caught my attention. She was quite a bit older than he, who knew how much older because Hypatia's precise date of birth has never been known. She was celibate, or at least that's what her contemporaries thought, and they believed she died an aged virgin. She was studious, a great teacher and sorcerer, mathematician, astronomer, philosopher and follower of the doctrines of Plato, Jamblico, and Plotinus; and considered by many to be a pagan. And Sinesio, a young Christian who in his own land achieved the high office of bishop, and it is probable that he wrote his last letters to Hypatia by a lamp on the same table that held the Gospels, still dressed in the insignia of his rank, tired of saying mass to the faithful, overwhelmed by the wars of his city and by his theological doubts, because even by the time the years had turned him bald he never stopped feeling like the young man who liked to hunt with his friends and loved Greek culture, and had never forgotten his teacher's house where he'd studied the ancient philosophers with dedication and had spoken of the procedures of dark and magic secrets not destined for just any ear. Of this correspondence, we have seven letters from Sinesio to Hypatia but none written by her to the student who until his death distinguished himself above all the other rich and brilliant young men who frequented her. Hypatia, who responded punctually to Sinesio in letters now lost to history, is the woman who tried to cure of his passion for her another of her disciples by rudely showing him a rag bloodied by her menstruation. Why then, this written dialog so long sustained? And what went on between them before Sinesio was called back to his country to occupy the elevated religious position he held until his death? This

correspondence lasted for years between the majestic blond matron, growing old with dignity in what was left of the library that was the reason for her existence and the beautiful student, adolescent at first and young man later, Libyan of slanted eyes and date-colored skin, hair like snakes and feline smiles, who walked silently among the stacks, his head slightly inclined above one shoulder in the same pose we see in Alexander's bust, his gaze lost in who knows what dreams as he recited stanzas of the Phedro.

It anguishes me that I will never learn in all their profundity the characters and personalities of the great women about whom I have written or wish to write. They all appear to me behind that veil of ingenious insolence that hides half their souls. They cultivate the enigma with a certain malice, a certain delight in tricking those who attempt to penetrate their mystery. Perhaps it is one last act of spectral flirtation they throw out from the halls of Death, the only thing their shadows eager for flesh still allow them, sighing...

Dear teacher

How might she have begun her letters in response to this tender claim? Perhaps she wrote *Dearly beloved disciple...*, or *Adored Sinesio....* We'll never know, short of some miracle.

If I could turn time back and surreptitiously enter Hypatia's body—that body her contemporaries have described as Olympic in the magnificent purity of its lines—, I would take that sentiment to its ultimate consequences which, I suspect, her heart held for the young Libyan. I would have satiated my body's desire and my spirit's hunger for tenderness, I would have leapt all barriers. In any case her abstinence did not efficiently protect her honor, and for some of her biographers, especially those of the Christian faith, she made the young man her lover, and they even insist that she had others; they accused her of being licentious as they believed all pagans were. And especially pagans from Alexandria, the world's second capital in pomp, riches, and commercial dynamism, and celebrated for its licentiousness. So much so, that Saint Clement, patriarch of the Church, had to advise

his flock on how to dress and conduct themselves at the banquets, so they would not resemble the uncouth and alcoholic Alexandrians who, with their sumptuous clothes stained in wine, corollas of fine gold in hair thick with grease, and shamelessly painted faces, lay randomly among themselves, boys with girls, male with female and sex with sex, everyone dancing, singing and falling over each other, following the musicians who animated the banquet hall and ending up in a line with the guests, who soon moved like a serpent among the palm groves, sunken in one mad collective copulation that filled the air with snorts, wails, laments and all manner of filthy sounds that betrayed the soul blinded by an excess of lewd and devilish practices. But, what would an enemy fail to say to one he repudiates, envies, or loves with an unproductive and sterile love that has rotted in the interstices of his heart?

I know Hypatia grew up caressed by the coldness of ancient marbles, the only eyes looking at her young body were the whites of the statues with which the Greeks adorned their palaces, and it was kissed only by the salty breezes that reached her window from the city's two ports. Only the lighthouse lamp washed over her sleeping skin in the depth of the Alexandrian night. Hypatia was as cold and chaste as the white moon, a god she may have loved. I, in her body, would have opened my bedroom doors and parted the tenuous canopy to receive Sinesio's trembling flesh against my own, Sinesio: that strong youth whose armpits held the scent of myrtle and whose skin was as firm as glass sweetly polished by the sea.

How many times would I have allowed beautiful Sinesio to enter the warmth of my belly like a savage orphan mollusk? Just once, to prove that divine ecstasy exists on Earth and is not only provoked by union with the One, and so I might sew that instant in my memory like a form of Eternity? Or perhaps many times, all those necessary to calm his passion and my own...? Who knows. There are very passionate men who in bed behave like awkward fetuses or monsters who devour women's treasures without giving anything in return. How often have I myself thought that the only thing capable of prolonging Desire is to withhold the feast until desperation; that he suspects it exists, that he aspire to its scent, that he imagines textures and shapes,

colors and tastes, but cannot touch them. That he intuits but can never be sure. Because confirmation is death to love. In death one defines styles, Lezama said, and he also wrote *to define is to render ash*. I say *never is always*, and *always never*.

It is possible that Hypatia, a woman possessed of great wisdom and of an intuition capable of overcoming her lack of carnal experience, may have chosen to cultivate Sinesio's from afar, so he might outlive her, perhaps even so she might outlive death like a colossal work of art.

If I could only go back in time, I would have gone with Sinesio and my death would have been different. Maybe my young lover would have brought me a palace in a forest of date trees, would have caressed me in the moonlight morning after morning until another source of pleasure or other duties took him from my side. Or we might have chosen to flee on the worst of nights, a sudden storm in the waters of the port capsizing our ship, sending it to the rocky bottom, burying it among great fronds of algae and coral skeletons. And of course we mustn't forget the possibility that the two of us ended up crushed beneath the ruins of the Museióm, buried by the savage hordes of Christians that, from time to time, flooded Alexandria's streets, yelling with their eyes deranged and those distorted mouths so reminiscent of Gorgon's screams as she madly shook her serpentine hair. That is how they placed Jesus upon the remains of a grandeur they have never understood. Upon the footprint of a world that was perfect in its essential purity.

So I, a cadaver at times and at others weeping over Sinesio's body, would not have written a single letter. But I was never within Hypatia, and so I must let go of this game in which I possess him and he possesses me and we are an illiterate duo of lovers, so like all the world's lovers, who consume their fire without leaving a trail in the water or dust of their days.

And so I have refused him, he has left, we are far from one another and I suspect we will not see each other again. When a messenger brings the first of his pleas to my door, I take it in my trembling hand that hypocritically hides the tension in its fingers and run to my

room hiding it between the pleats of my tunic and the splendor of my sandals that fly over labyrinthine mosaic landscapes. Once in the safety of my room I press the letter against my breasts and kiss it again and again. Then I lay on the bed and avidly read one line, another, another.... An hour, perhaps two, pass before I rise, take the pen in my fingers made clumsy by emotion, dip it into my alabaster inkwell and its shadow moves across the blank white papyrus.

If I were Hypatia, how might I have begun my first response to Sinesio?

Sweet gift of the gods, brought to me like a pearl thrust by the sea upon the sands of Rakotis...

But I do not want to confess to him my sad love that allowed him to leave, my cowardly love that did not have the fortitude to show itself in time, and so I write:

Good Sinesio, adorned with all the gifts of intellect and spirit, may wisdom be with you...

It is hot and I am sweating. I know that today is Thursday, the third day of December, 2009. That it is eight at night and that before me I only have the yellow wall of my room, a computer on which I type these pages, a fan that refreshes Havana's gloom.... But I am not surprised when I raise my eyes and all that has disappeared, leaving in its place a great window with marble columns looking out upon the coast's lapping waters, and far off I see the light from a lighthouse, spinning round and round, casting its beam on my forehead and cheeks. Suddenly at midnight the cold wind strikes my skin, bringing me the smell of rotten fish and the sweat of drunken passersby on their way to make merry in some palace or other. My hand escapes my will and writes of its own accord:

You should know, Sinesio, that this afternoon when the prefect Orestes was at the theater issuing a decree on the representation

of pantomimes, a brawl broke out among Greeks, Egyptians and Christians, each on their own and all together against the Jews, who screamed that Cirilo's agents were agitating the public. You know that the Jews of Alexandria enjoy Tome's protection since the time of Cesar, and Orestes decided to hear their complaints. The Jews demanded the demise of Hierax, that Alexandrian teacher devoted to Cirilo, do you remember him? To my surprise and disgust, Orestes ignored my advice and ordered Hierax be captured and tortured. Cirilio called in the Jewish leaders and threatened them. That night Saint Alexander church went up in flames, and when the Christians tried to put out the fire, a troop of Jews attacked them, massacring many. An hour later Cirilo arrived in the Jewish quarter with his people enraged. He ordered that all the property of its inhabitants be confiscated and began expelling them from the city. Orestes arrived with his Roman guards, but one of the five hundred fanatical monks who Cirilo recently brought from the Nitrian desert threw a stone at the prefect and shattered his skull. Orestes commanded he be tortured and he died. They say he was called Amonio, like Plotinio's teacher, and that he was young and of a passionate nature. In Alexandria the situation is very difficult, and I fear truly horrible things will happen over the next few days. These are not the commotions to which we have been accustomed up to now. The Christians have gained in strength and Cirilo possesses neither scruples nor measure.

You have done well to leave. I too would leave if I did I not have to watch over the Museión's manuscripts and maps, all we have left of Alexandria's library. I cannot abandon the wisdom that was deposited in my care. And so I will remain here, although now I am hated because of my friendship with the prefect Orestes. Cirilo has gotten his people to believe that Orestes obeys me in everything, that he has succumbed to my witch's enchantments. I pray to the gods, and I hope the Universe will reach out to protect this its servant, and that the stars will dim so that Cirilo cannot find his way to me. You pray too, good

Sinesio, so the gods will allow me to live out my natural life and I may be able to continue bringing the light of true knowledge and thought to mankind. I feel like a gladiator fighting a lonely battle in the circus arena, pursued by hundreds of wild beasts hiding in the shadows and of which I cannot see more than the malignant brilliance of their eyes.

Of course, I will not tell him that with a bag of coins I bought an ancient papyrus found among the tombs at Oxirrynco. It contains an immortality ritual based upon formulae from a time in which the assassin Osiris was nothing more than a huge serpent coiled in the shadowy depth of a cave. I cannot confess to him that I do not want to die, and that along with that papyrus I also purchased a dark and beautiful slave to impregnate my virgin womb. I feel death approach and wish to leave something of myself in this world, a little soul who can continue caring for the Museión and all the manuscripts we've been taking for months to the desert caves. They will remain there until everything is finished. For centuries if need be, and the world has been freed from the Cirilos and dark monks who do not believe in philosophy's divine light.

With this letter, I am sending you a copy in gold of The Caldeo Manuscripts *we so often studied together in the golden afternoons of my garden. I want you to keep them among your books. Nothing that is true can offend your faith in the Crucified One. I only want you to remember me when I am nothing more than a painful shadow of Averno. I cannot live, Sinesio, very much longer....*

I think for a moment and then add that I have received his letter, the one in which he told me about the hydrometer's construction, and I will write that I enthusiastically congratulate him for his efforts on its behalf. And only then will I go on to mention a delicate subject:

You will no doubt hear, from many mouths, the news of my mar-
riage to the philosopher Isidoro, whom you met at my house. The
prefect Orestes advised me to marry so I would have a husband's
protection, as well as that of the personal guard he so generously
puts at my disposition each time I leave my palace. Isidoro is
with me, as my husband. At night he inhabits the opposite wing
of my house, from where one can see the apple orchard in which
you and I walked so often....

Yes, I must somehow tell him that the pathway to my womb that I have denied him is also denied all other men. Love would have taken me from my studies and tied my feet to the ground, and I do not know if love's fruits would have tasted as good as the fruits of philosophy have, nor if they'd have lasted as long.... Consummated love is as ephemeral as the spurious light of the stars.

The port's lamp blinds me with its splendor. I think that when Sinesio, at his palace in Sirene, wrote his last letter to me, he couldn't have known precisely what his fingers traced. At the very instant in which he began his letter by calling me *the most sensible and venerated of all philosophers*, he could not have known, had no way of knowing that he was writing to carrion already smoldering on the embers of a trash heap on the outskirts of Alexandria. Perhaps at the very moment in which Sinesio was writing to me in the loneliness of his studio, and a melancholy smile flowered on his lips, destiny had already decided that the Lector Peter and Cirilo's bitter monks were murdering me on the altar of the Caesarium, and that their dirty claws, which just that morning had blessed the water beneath the Cross, ferociously skinned my naked limbs with sharp ceramic blades, pieces of the Library shelves demolished by their axes. How fortunate that your soul already departed, Sinesio, and you cannot know what happened on my way to give a lecture at the Museión this morning. A mob of Christians gathered in front of my house and, as I emerged, became rowdier, more menacing, and ended up throwing stones at my carriage, stabbing my slaves and, pushing and pulling me by the hair, dragging me to the stone altar at the church where in ancient times the Alexandrians

surreptitiously worshiped César. Now they hit me, angrily tear me apart, and for a few seconds I am able to see their beastly faces covered with dirty beards, and their dark tunics beginning to soak up my warm red blood. In one blow Pedro tears out one of my ribs and holds it up, a triumphant trophy before the eyes of his followers. Now all of them together drag what is left of me. I suffer atrocious pain as the mob emits its fiery shrieks. One of my thighs, its flesh softened and sunken from age, breaks at one end, the arteries hanging out, separates from my hip and remains trapped among some stones. My mutilated body. That same body my father Teón formed at academies and polished in the baths of my palace so it would become a living temple of Ideas. Each moment I am more a mass of shredded meat, quartered, blackened. And now I am thrown into the Cinaron's fire. Now I burn, my Sinesio! Now I am flame, I am Light!

I didn't have time to reveal my sentiments to you. I curse such silence. Unspoken passion is condemned to Nothingness. But with the last breath that escapes my lips, on the wings of my soul transformed into a butterfly that manages to escape the pyre, I send you my last letter, where I do not tell you of my agony but where I evoke for you the memory of one of our most complicit and tender moments: that night when, embracing, we contemplated the blossoming of lotus flowers in my garden pool...

To the brightest and most beloved of men. Look, oh Sinesio, at how the shadow of a cloud on the water approaches the moon....

Lourdes González

The Voices of Alma Rubens

I have been too accommodating. I must insist. I must explode this town in pieces. I must go naked to the house of the timid one, the cheat, the insolent. Naked, so his eyes will see freedom. And still, I have only created myself anew. My body has become the palace in which news of the past is performed.

At moments, between the walls of the house, I remember the willingness of our best youths, those for whom the world is nothing more than a stage on which to dance, dance, let fly the arrow that pierces an ever more distant horizon. All preceded by the white mist of infancy, that only comes in three vacuous scenes, meaning nothing yet.

And I don't know if my voice remains that of the excited young girl who provoked small scandals among pompous literary groups or if, standing firm, José Manuel Poveda used me from his *non plus ultra*, from the infernal eternity surely consumed by laughter and blasphemy. No, it is absurd to imagine that a single voice accompanies one throughout one's life. Sometimes I fall into the trap of monotonous authenticities, my voice has changed, it has greater control, is more sacrificial because I am more sacrificial. The slavery of intemperance bored me.

To be honest I must say that my triumphs were always linked to certain desires of body and soul. When I could combine these, the solution and rest were comforting; if I was only able to achieve one of the two, my disobedience got the better of me. But I had a great many satisfactions, and I knew several poets, Poveda's followers, who continue to be the best way of reaching me. Angel Escobar is a good example.

I wasted many nights and days, but in all that delirium, along with the horror of the being who accompanied me, there was always

a pale light among those that emerged at dawn, a sign of resistance, a weak response to my questions.

Ninety-six was my worst year. It seemed like the last room's threshold, one foot struggling to reach the next step and the other searching in the air for an opportunity of survival and elevation.

Throughout its days, and during all the days of the next two years, I sustained a difficult conversation with the world. More difficult, much more difficult, than when I explored the senses. I suddenly felt that unreality no longer belonged to me and I immersed myself in a *pleat of calamities* for which I did not prove sufficient. I must confess that's how I learned the word *surprise*, and when I did I had to remain seated for a few minutes at a spot on the bridge that crosses a miserable river in order to survive somehow and get where I am now. Those fragments of past lives beside the black water of a bad-smelling arroyo were in and of themselves a great spiritual war, a great depression that moved me definitively.

The news was terrible, and we were also hungry, we all wanted to smell of daffodils, we all wanted to use blue money. The three of us gathered in the living room, surrounded by darkness, to decide what we would sell of the family's belongings. We spoke in single syllables and silences. I have never been closer to Poveda's stature than at that time when he offered me his mercy.

In the end, I was nothing more than a provincial poet's illusion of freedom, the feminine voice of a man filled with the absolute, a spendthrift, an egomaniac. I have also never asked for more than to comply with the satisfaction that he himself sensed when he wrote my lines.

Surrounded by walls we invented a way to postpone the end, we opened a family business in which even the knives sounding in the bottoms of the plates reminded us of our lost intimacy. We survived. We paid the boatman with our dream and the boatman accepted. When his figure was filled with shadow, Poveda convoked my name in the sacred name of the Word, and I had to write all the details of the event once more, in the female voice he favored. I traded the now public *Misery, mud, vile resentments, old blasphemies, unconfessed sins, guilty desires, deep black murky water, hidden in the depths of one's being. Beaten*

*psyche, oh, abyss of tepid vice without shame, recipient of all that is absent and lost...nothing in nothingness, nothing in which the gods themselves are nothing...*for new expressions such as: *As simply as that we began this game of deconstructing the house, one stone after another, so we could eat. When nothing was left, I occasionally sold myself, but it wasn't enough and so we sold the door; then we sat down, decided to stop playing that game to live in what was left of the house and play a more terrible game: we decided to sell all our time, and eat.*

It wasn't the same era, it couldn't have been the same plot, I had to tell myself that true voice is simply another illusion, that we are really speaking of voices, the soul is plural. Poveda confirmed it. The final victory was saving the house, and eating so we could arrive at this moment when I can describe the events of the shipwreck once more.

Of course, it's not about a life fragmented by those terrible *special years*, I have had other dark moments of intense loneliness, extreme confusion, exhaustion, free will. The shipwreck was only the climax.

One afternoon in 1972, one I don't believe was calmer or any less calm than today, on the balcony of a building that was Santiago de Cuba's first military barracks, by then reduced to a dirty jumble of rooms, I looked down on the features of the inner courtyard where tall black women washed long pieces of cloth. Suddenly the grass turned savage, the smell of mud rising from the cement, upon which soldiers had marched so long before, intensified, the heat produced an alert state, and in an instant I understood the vague sensation of power that goes along with writing. I wouldn't be able to define that moment, I never have, not even accompanied as I am by a poet of Poveda's talent.

Later I no longer wanted to go on, for thirteen years I hid behind a few poems. My return was magical but stunning, to go back to depending on words when I hoped to achieve greater pleasures, to remember everything once more, translate it into the language of the senses and inscribe it upon a delicate white page.

But I returned. I retrieved the practice of jotting down opinions, sensations and emotions, to accommodate them, situate them, dismember them, make cause for them, invent poems. The halves and urgencies became whole in fleeting spaces that supported them for

several days, later dissipating in difficult rupture. I did what Poveda would have done: I resisted the Word once more. And thanks to that I could later tell what I have told here, and a few other stories, even those I come to in the unquiet loneliness of my room.

Now I look through the haze of years, and its glow, I see the lines of beloved bodies, I evoke the amber noontimes of devastations, observe the swans. The lines of my hands still belong to my name and that is the unmistakable sign that Poveda was right when he summoned me to the dangerous and alienating work of writing. He was also correct in imposing a method: to live, to live first, to love first, to first create what you love, to observe the nets, to extend yourself to their edges, take stock of the bilge, give yourself to those furies of time that are yours, allow your heart to understand and, later, before you heal the wounds, before the fires burn out, before you attempt to calm yourself: write. Before scent, delight, scenes and dreams disappear from memory, write them all.

Canicular summer, 2009

Manelic R. Ferret

File

"And who is this creature?" I ask, my eyes on the false ceiling. The radio responds "for you, *La vie en rose*" by the one and only Edith Piaf. I raise the volume all the way, let those passersby who are surely out there hear it and fill themselves with hope. An incredible green scent fills the air. I stop before a long mirror, the right side of my face literally crystallized. My right eye is no longer my right eye, nor is it in its usual place. I myself am no longer in my usual place. Someone come to my aid, someone has turned on the radio. I look at this room: a toilet without a door, a plastic chair barricading the blinds, an Inpud fan. Inpud is the best. Just like Coppelia. Cuban music is also the best. And Caribe televisions. But Suchel, for example, was discreet until he joined Camacho, a Spanish woman, or a Mexican, I can't remember. Brazil came along and provided an alternative to our domestic cigarettes, they added a filter and wrapped them in sweetened sugarcane papers: *Populares* for half a dollar. We are America's Searchlight and this has nothing to do with the blackouts; it belongs to a higher plane. I return to the personal: a little unknown creature waking up in an unknown room after a profound mental block caused by various external injuries. I find my bag on the floor and pick it up. I go through it and see a pair of little cigars, a card with a likeness of the Vigin of the Caridad del Cobre and another of Pablo Escobar. A small notebook. A strange piece of paper that says "Mane owes me 25 dollars pay up you shit or I'll kill you." And another "on June 8th I received this curious threat...." The rest, almost illegible poems. A book: *Latin American Love Poems* by Mario Benedetti. An identity card: Mane Ferret, Santiago de Cuba 21-9-1961, daughter of Héctor and Egda. That's me, although I don't remember Héctor...nor Egda. I'm hungry. I'm always hungry.

A small dried out rose in my pocket. I pick up my bag and go out into the street.

This head full of boleros, feet that trip over the great roots that buckle the sidewalks. A shadow replaces me on those sidewalks. I see myself go, crossing the city that swallows one's footsteps out of the shadows. So absurd is the Absurd, everything relegated: *Club Le Select* defines selectivity and you are excluded. The faint breeze wants to settle. I note once again your absence beside me. Once and again your absence of irreversibly no longer loving me, so that I wander like this, carrying my difference through the streets. You and Havana, neither of you are for me. As simple as life itself: the problem isn't being a woman, or being black, or being a woman from Santiago, from the "interior;" these are others' problems. The problem is you, Darsita My Love, you've left me hanging onto God's hand, like a piece of dry grapefruit or lemon peel. My problem isn't this background I drag about like an iron box. Take one look at the iron box: inside is my infancy, like anyone of my generation, parents who divorced and give themselves to their work; grandmother's cream skirt; a love like any other adolescent love except it was for my biology professor who also strangely took note of me, bestowing my first kiss as I slept on the cot beside her son. Our separation was wild: Egda took her pistol and threatened the universe. Double suicide: she committed suicide and I did too. At home, they also don't know who this creature is. That small female family—Lorca's people, Grandmother, Mother, Aunt, they don't know anything. But it's all so clear it isn't even a problem; there are so many non-problems like this: I was fifteen when a child was born in the house, and a bit older when that child recognized me forever, but could never cuddle with me, take walks, make puppets, the Aunt cared jealously for her baby: almost everyone thinks I'm contagious.

Until I could finally participate in the rain outside my window and grow into the University. Early morning hours dragging guitars and alcohol, Casagranda Roof Garden, San Pedro del Mar, Rancho Club, heard our songs, "please, would you sing *Antonio's Woman...*? until the poet Heredia sheltered us in the intimacy of his patio. An

academy for the revolutionaries of the eighties, and a wedding in '81.... Wait a moment: that guy who was my friend, introducing himself to the startled eyes of the Grandmother, the Aunt, the Mother, with a false doctor's certificate, my name linked to a supposed abortion. I don't know why they wouldn't believe me and that stranger suddenly assuming my life: two months fighting against his power, violation, fear, and the Emptiness, the country bumpkin only took notice when I let a coal iron fall on his head, the violence within me, like I've already said, it's metabolic. After that, only now have I once again tasted such unlimited spaces of Emptiness, nevertheless I feel very strong this time. At Literature School, since I've never thought of any other, there wasn't only literature but stones, spit at other young people who were leaving the country, drastic solutions by Cubans who burned themselves in Granada embracing the flag, Palestinian students who never returned from vacation and became photos, cannon fodder of the moment. And I'm not telling you to believe, I'm telling you just read this and only this. Six years at the University wasn't a problem.

We must pay for all that good stuff we've received. I went to pay for mine at a place I'd never heard of: Bartolomé Masó. The debt is called Social Service, such a beautiful name. I saw myself in that vile place that people there called Be Masó for short. A Pedagogical Documentation and Information Center in the wilderness: no student ever showed up to document herself or ask for information. Pastimes to choose from, at the Tiburón, a skein of beer and real macho men with machetes at their waists, an enriching experience. On Wednesdays, I would go to a bakery at Cauto Cristo to teach Grammar to an old baker who waited for me ashamed of his age and ignorance, begging me: "Pass me, Teacher, I need the grade so I can get an electric fan." The fact that that old man could only earn a fan at the age of sixty if he passed Spanish isn't a problem: *struggle* exists in Cuba. You spend your life struggling for the slightest material thing, anything is valid. You're finished if you don't have a talent for struggle. You must struggle for food, clothing, a light bulb, deodorant. An electric fan. You can't get any necessity easily. But this is an understood aspect of life since 1959, no one complains, not me, since your spirit

is guaranteed, and so there's no problem here. He gave me a piece of bread and I wasn't so strict when I graded his final exam.

After those three interminable years in the place with the beautiful name, there was only one place I wanted to see, Havana; there's nowhere else. I came with my things, my song, my words. But here neither Sindo Garay nor Matamoros matter; Guillén was a pig about whom they used the terrible adjective corny: decadent, clichéd, cheap, out of style. I hung up my corny guitar and let my words carry another music, surreptitiously. I'd already slept in hospitals, bus and train stations, airports, morgues, on rooftops...always beneath the elements in winter, in summer, in September.

No one wants my books; no one knows who this creature is who continues to wander the Only City. And along those byways that come and go I found it. I no longer remembered my thousand former loves, Berta's cruelty, Luisa's death, not even Liset's breasts. It all ceased being a problem. Twenty-eight years to be born and live everything with abandon, making delicious mistakes without models, remodeling myself, all by instinct, extreme. The infinite Special Period that devastate(d) the country passed over us and wasn't a problem, nor the scarcity, nor the sea covered with precarious rafts in that sad year that was 1994, that massive exodus, each individual condemning him- or herself, electing to be part of the sordid mass. My experience of living with someone lasted seven years. Seven: the number of light, of taking off, only she didn't understand or didn't experience it as I did. On long slow feet, she left. She didn't even turn her head or give me a decent goodbye. For me, the shock of the universe, a galactic loneliness, and back to the fiction, this parody of life. A mourning of grass, a sweet mourning and light rain on earth: the tree is dead. Its leaves lay in the sun without the lethal holes caused by its branches. There is no flotation line, just a furious ray, zigzagging. I feel geniuses calling at my door: I open wide, my chest constricted: it is the thunder, I have seen the violence of the light that will precede it, the next time, in identical repetition, but will it call at my door then?

I feel a beat swelling in the Emptiness, a unique essence in the middle of that vulgar totality built around the Emptiness. I go along

the street panting, looking for shade, frightened of the visible and imaginary that have their own colors, their own velocity, eyes: *we are what's left/ what sells like warm bread....* Who could trouble herself like that for love, poet's karma, centuries of the same thing, *what people prefer and ask for/ what sells out at the market,* from Má Teodora to now, this Island's habitual behavior, they call it an Archipelago: it's historically impossible to dream of some conciliatory temperament, rather stain as if with soot *what we hear everywhere: we are the best, the biggest.*[8]

The only thing left to me was to drag my feet to El Baluarte, where magic reins, to look for the definitive answer, to consult the Highest Disciple. I walked along the sea, expectant, fearing and longing for the sentence that would be revealed to me. I thought of Sor Juana, of Ibarbouri, of Agustini, and I thought of Violeta Parra, searching for strength and reaffirmation beyond this earthly plane. The High Disciple carried out her ritual on the table—her eyes lost to me behind the arabesque of her scarf—, and thought a few minutes before responding. First that *infinite* gaze, I don't know if toward other lives, then the gesture of her hand, and finally the Word in a single phrase: —But not now.

8 *What We Are,* by Manolín, *El Médico de la Salsa,* a subject that always reminds me of Whitman.

Yannis Lobaina

Juana of León, That's Me

To my beloved city of Baracoa

It's been twenty years since I've left the house. I'm afraid of sunlight, I'm afraid people will insult me, point at me with their dirty fingers, and say: "Look at her, Juana de León," and then I'd have to listen to their laughter and hurtful comments. That's why I didn't tell you when I married Miguel Chicoy. What for? So I'd be on the lips of every inhabitant of the city of Asunción de Baracoa?

It's been a while since my name is no longer Juana de León, but Juana the disgraced one. I'm almost sixty years old and the people of this city hate me. There are times I want to die, I can no longer bear this life of lies, of hypocrisy. My few friends have moved to the capital and my family is dead. I'm alone, alone on this earth. No one understands me, no one forgives what I did. Yes, it all happened a long time ago.

Sometimes I wish the earth would open up and swallow me, and that I would no longer have to remember that day, that day, when I married Enrique and consented to living beneath her roof. Yes, I knew. I knew she was a woman, she herself had told me so. But I loved her, I respected her, and that was all that mattered to me. Imagine the shame my mother would have felt if she'd learned that her daughter had married a woman the same as her. My God, she never would have forgiven me, just thinking about that makes me want to die. Everyone says I'm crazy.

Chicoy has imprisoned me at the top of the city, in a place called Paradise; but it's like hell. It's far from everyone, only a few neighbors around, near the cemetery. The earth around here is red like blood, the hill steep like all the pain I still carry within me. I live with the

great thorn of shame piercing my throat, all because I didn't defend Enrique. I carry her like the Parra cross, hard and heavy on my back.

But today I will fervently ask Saint John to forgive me, I want to die in peace. I've never known peace, all those voices of the city insulting me, cursing me, engraved in my head since that morning of the trial, up to now the most scandalous on the Island. The look on her face as they judged her, imploring me to tell the truth. The truth? What is the truth?

I never manage to sleep, never. I am always sick. Some days I hear Enrique's sweet voice and it's so loud and real that I must close myself in my room for fear that my husband will hear it too. I hide beneath the bed, and we talk there for hours. I often fall asleep beneath the bed, and between the heat and thinking of Enrique...I awake soaked in sweat. Several days may pass, and I still hear that voice whispering in my ears. I carry her contagious laughter in the deepest part of myself. Now and then the memory of one or another of our days together surprises me, just she and I in the room, when she helped me braid my long hair, always such a tangle. And sometimes, when I take a bath, I can feel Enrique's slender fingers, forever helping me. Because of my sickness, I was barely able to do it by myself. Then, sweetly, she would scratch my back with her delicate nails, and observe my skin for a long time. She said I was beautiful, and that my skin shone like obsidian.

I think today is the day on which I will tell everyone the true story of my life. In this city, everyone thinks I am crazy, and no one listens to me, but I want the young people of this cursed place to know the truth about Juana de León. Some will say: and what's she getting at now, if she can't change anything...but telling my story will help me die in peace.

I suddenly remember that I am the same as this city: disgraced and cursed. "It's a shame, with how beautiful the city is, and with the fertility of its land, that it is surrounded by water and so far from the capital. We should go to the big city, Juanita," that's what Enrique used to tell me, and I should have listened, she repeated it often enough.... But I never wanted to listen to her. I wanted to stay in my city.

I never believed she truly loved me. Nor did I imagine she would be able to leave everything behind to begin a life with me. She begged again and again that we go to Havana, and said: "Juanita, in the capital no one will know our story. We can be happy." But I didn't want to listen to her. Today I wanted to cook something that reminds me of Enrique. Wherever she may be, I want her to know I am very repentant. I will cook thinking of her. Teti with white rice, the scent of that small fish reminds me of the first time she came to my shack, and I was making lunch, a delicious Teti stew, with fresh tomatoes, picked from my own little garden. Enrique brought me herbs, garlic, onions, and I added cilantro, she didn't know that leaf until she tasted it with me. She told me she would never forget its scent. And she embraced me.

I remember it was Sunday and my two brothers, my godmother and I were together preparing a good weekend meal. When she arrived, we told her what was in the pot. She left satisfied. That was the first time I saw her, after that she began visiting often. She said she wanted to help me. I was frequently ill, convulsed by fevers. She said we lived very far from the village, that one day I would die and there wouldn't be enough time to get help. I remember she asked me to marry her again and again, to help me. She said she would teach me to read and write, and if I wanted even other languages.

I began to think that I was delirious from so much fever. I couldn't understand her, it was too much luck for a poor peasant woman. Although it's true, Enrique made it clear that we should be friends first, that a relationship should first be based on friendship, and she said she would never ever touch me if I didn't want her to.

One August night, shortly before our marriage, I went to bed with a crisis of fever, and Enrique was by my side all day. She cared for me as if I were her daughter, she brought my food to the bed, she combed my hair and washed me. That night as she put the cold compresses on my forehead, a few drops of water spilled onto my breasts, and she carefully dried them. At one of those moments I felt her breath choked with emotion, a scent like mint with patchouli coming from her mouth. We continued looking into each other's eyes, hers sparkled and I pulled her closer until my mouth was on hers and we

kissed one another, a long kiss. Sometimes the fevers make me delirious. But no, that day I knew what I was doing, and we kissed again several times, late at night when everyone else slept, those long kisses of ours. That was the way it was for several months. And I agreed. That day, before the judge, I was such a coward, I felt so ashamed of myself, that I didn't know what to do, what to say. I know that was the day I lost her forever.

Ah, but she also shared in the guilt of our discovery. She was very creative and loved to kid around. So one day she invented an apparatus that imitated a male sex organ, she put it on and showed it to the mayor of Tiguabos so he might document the fact that she was a man.

I wanted to die the day she came home laughing and smelling of drink, and told me that story. I told her several times to get rid of that thing and she vowed she would. But she didn't. One night Enrique wanted us to sleep together. It was cold and I agreed. I could hardly sleep. I felt her warm body next to mine and that breath of mint with patchouli I liked so much. I didn't know what to do, and then I turned around and kissed her.

Yes, I admit that I liked playing with Enrique, and that the two of us were happy in our games. I will confess everything. Today I want to feel the peace I haven't felt for twenty years. I want to die without having to feel I didn't tell the truth. Yes, I know, it's late. She is gone and I am old and alone. It doesn't matter. It's true she was very strange, but I must say it, I achieved a pleasure with her I have never had with my husband Chicoy. I think he's always known it, and that's why he's imprisoned me at the top of the city, far from everyone. He always told me he wouldn't let me go out because my fever was contagious. He separated me from my few friends. And the nearest neighbors wouldn't even look at me. Everyone thought I was ill and that Faber's spirit would return to me.

Every time I think of that trial: me standing there, in front of her, she looking at me with her little blue eyes, her small red mouth, asking me to tell the truth. And I didn't say anything, I acted as if I didn't know anything, I said she never told me, that she tricked me, and I lied even more: I said she touched me once. When I said that

my mouth got dry and my words felt empty, my eyes got wet and there was a lot of talking in the courtroom. The judge had to shout to make it stop. After that huge lie, I felt miserable.

I am miserable. I should shout it out, so I can feel I've done something. I will escape when Chicoy isn't looking, and I will go to the ceremony the city is offering to Saint John, today June 24th. Everyone goes from the city single file, to the nearest rivers: the Toa or the Duaba. They celebrate their rituals to the saint at the mouths of those rivers. They say it helps purify the soul, that it cleanses you of all your guilt. I need that today. I need that ritual a thousand times over. My life has been a beehive of guilt for twenty years. There's not a day I don't think of Enrique, in what they must have done to her.... I don't know if she has been able to escape her prison, or if she has been able to go back to her country. Some say she wanders the streets of Santiago, others say Havana.

The truth is, on days like this I think of her and all the questions in the world assault me, I think of delicate Faber, her beauty, how kind she was to me, and how I treated her in return. My chest constricts, it's hard to breathe when I think of that sunny afternoon, when she took me to her house, vulnerable and alone. My God, sometimes one doesn't know how one act can do so much damage, we aren't conscious that a single word can bring down a mountain.

I must lose my fear of people and join the crowd. I will walk to the Duaba River, so my guilt will settle. I heard the spiritualist Lucrecia say that. The city of Asunción is almost dead. You can barely hear the faithful, the sound of the sea doesn't even reach the city, every day Baracoa's streets fill with dust, and the people too and their red-roofed houses. Everything is losing its color. I can barely see the colors of the rich landowners' houses. Where has everyone gone? They say to Santiago. Baracoa is no longer the place where people come to sell their wares. I am afraid, everything is so dirty, the odor of dried fish invades the city, people are sad because they say they are going to tear the church down.

My poor city of Baracoa, sinking into the sea, into misery. That guy they call crazy, el Pelú, already said it: "It will be poor as long as it

exists." Dear God, I hope that's not true. I wouldn't want to be forced to leave my place, my small country. I would like to die in it, return where I was born. Poor as I am, I want to die in Asunción de Baracoa.

Yes, I know what they think. That I'm crazy. Very crazy. Maybe they will throw stones at me on my way to the river. It doesn't matter. I'm short of breath and my eyes can barely distinguish those who make fun of me, my pulse hardly allows me to make a dish of teti with white rice. I can still hear her defense attorney, Doctor Manuel Vidaurre, telling us: "Enriqueta Faber is not a criminal. The city is guiltier than she is, from the moment they denied women their civil and political rights, making them into objects of men's pleasure."

As my footsteps don't seem to take me very far, my body is already on the shore of the Duaba River. I dip my head into the water and shout as loud as I can: "Saint John, forgive me. My dear Enriqueta, come back!"

Ruth Behar

Eternity

I've forgotten how to write a poem.

No one believes me.

But it's true.

They gave me a big prize. The Cervantes. It arrived too late. They awarded it to a woman who has let the ink in her pen go dry.

Every day now I receive a visitor at five in the afternoon. The hour of Lorca and all the poets. She comes to see the poet who inhabits the ruins of a palace without words.

I am going blind, so the ruins don't bother me. I'm happy living among shadows.

Visitors come and sit beside me and speak. They think I am listening, when the truth is they bore me. I close my eyes and dream of other cities. Madrid. Cairo. Istanbul.

I'm not one to eat that much. I've always wanted to live on air and pollen like a hummingbird.

I don't know what's wrong with me.

I have a bottomless hunger.

My niece tells me there's no food in Havana. There's nothing. No sweet-smelling soap, no white meat, no fresh milk. She talks about The Special Period. I have no idea what she's talking about.

I am hungry. For the first time.

A North American woman who says she's from Cuba has come to the house. She brought her poems so I can critique them. She says I inspired her. I asked her to read them out loud. Her Spanish is broken. But she gets her meaning across. Her poems might be better, although they aren't terrible.

Innocently, she asks me what advice I can give her as a poet. I tell her to read more and write less.

What I like is that she brings me cookies like those from before. That's why I have allowed her to come to see me several times and read her poems again and again.

She has brought me cookies of different flavors—chocolate with honey, Turkish almonds and even ginger. As soon as she says goodbye, I call my niece and tell her to open the package and put the cookies on a plate. I eat them all, slowly, one by one. Well, almost all, because my niece takes the plate away before I've finished the last of them, telling me I'll get sick from eating so many sweets.

My niece doesn't understand that those cookies give me energy to go on living. I even feel the desire to sit down and write a poem, one as long as a love letter.

The cookies are so good. I wish we had a bit of black tea, the kind the Russians used to send, to eat them with a cup of steaming liquid. But I'm not complaining. The cookies, just by themselves, are a blessing.

Could I start writing? Let's see if I can write another poem like "Eternity." That is the poem people like best, the most famous of them all. I wrote it in fifteen minutes, maybe less. It was so easy to write back then.

Now I'm old. I don't think of eternity any more, but of what flavor of cookies that North American girl will bring next time, that North American who was once a child in Cuba.

Havana, March 9, 2013

Gertrudis Ortiz

Me, that One, Myself

(Theater Piece)

All the sailors and vagabonds in the world, welcome to this port. Come on in, irrelevant alcoholics, depressed ones, patriots on their way into exile, husbands saying goodbye. Come on, come on, look at this face blushing for immortality. How are you doing? It's good to see ourselves the way we are. What's the use of those who arrive being shown any old truth? Which one? This childlike face surprised by life, this picture, me, that one, that very one... Am I real?

We already know that nothing resembles a face more than a mask, I didn't have to wait a whole century to say so. Every life is an imitation. Poets tell us that. Mine may be the least important. I put on the mask of a woman without history: a woman who serves others, who returns home alone on full moon nights as well as in the insecurity of the storm, and sleeps by herself, her face to the wall.

What do I have to tell? The discussions with my mother. —Useless! she said. The way I went out walking at the port, fleeing her repetitions, and my flight not wishing to repeat her history of a woman who was also alone, because her husband laughs with other women only to return to his bed at dawn so he can be a good father, a good worker, a good, good...

There, here is my rage and your guilt, incipient painter of dances, the circus, theaters, whores. I fell a little bit in love with you! How sad! How lonely, you have syphilis La Roja gave you! Who left you for another, exploited you, laughed at you. I loved you. Let me take care of you, lame one, yesterday's drunk. Did you once aspire to happiness on Parisian streets? I swear to God, I would have loved you, ugly as you were, I'd never been to Paris.

Painter of interiors. Others, not mine. Childless woman, without a sharp pain in your belly from being open to the world, without shame, without sowing the seed of continuity.

I don't tell myself that. I am the flower of the Stard, she who you painted with blue shadows, the color of happiness. I hadn't complained up to now, but I celebrate one hundred years today, the right day to talk. I am posterity. Will I celebrate another hundred years? Will no one change my life?

Always with that sideways look: you gave me a glance unlike any I've known, but I am looking. I'm not going to be sorry for what I say. You painted me and fell in love with another, with the beautiful passenger on her way to meet her husband in Senegal. You painted me and touched her on the thigh. As if the spout of the coffee pot was shouting its warning to you: I am going out, I am going to split these seams once and for all.... Everything for another woman. Your passion wasn't for me, wasn't about me.

But I am a woman, and a woman is every woman. I go for the similarity, what the blind poet said about men: I will be luminous.

Moulin Rouge, Moulin Rouge,
pour qui mouds-tu, Moulin Rouge,
pour la mort ou pour l'amour?
pour qui mouds-tu jusqu'au jour?

Ay! I also drink today. My conscience keeps me up. They can touch my ass if they want, for a drink or for love. These hours are like leaving the everyday world, where there's little food and it's sometimes rotten.

What weighs on me now is a whole century's loneliness. Those who sell violets are alone in all the world's plazas; Tula was alone in Seville's rooms when she wrote to Tasara and to Cepeda; Ofelia sang sad songs in cold water, immersed in a crazed and tormented loneliness.

Ah! What do I have? The loneliness of a man and his friends, that important sign we always need. Almost all my friends left via

that port, to other lands, other skies, other dreams. I stayed here without them and bore up under every sort of frugality, dressed in any old thing; and they, under any flag, living sometimes generous lives. Scented shawls arrive for me; bright crayons; earrings; black tea, green, red, in pretty little boxes. Small bills arrive to solve my small problems. Better cheese, better ink, oils, olives...ah!

How often have I said goodbye? So alone, alone with the light of these colors, a life that even thrilled the painter, I want to ascend to another light. It wasn't always like this, illusions are worth something. I once had a man who taught me that stars have several ways of shining. He was a sailor, he drank mint liqueur, and invited me sweetly without offering money, to sigh on the docks. I went. I like real things. If you sigh without money passing hands it can be real. That's what I thought. Ah, men! From the moment he saw the sailor, the painter looked at me differently. I might have stopped being immortal, but it was just a moment, unsettling: I lay down with the sailor on the sand, we watched the balloons come and go, or we went to a clean guest house. That's right, I always demanded that: everything clean. I snuck from my brothers' room, from its acrid odor. For a while, in addition to a good looking sailor I had a place of my own, for me alone. I recognize that it took courage to escape my limits, but I became Dolly again: submissive, pretty, down at the port.

Tell me, bow-legged guy, is it moral to have only one husband to wash your back in the tub? Is what your uncle did moral, half-crazy with nobility: burn your nostalgic paintings of houses of ill repute and prostitutes at Malromé castle, of masturbations, of medical nudes...? Morality is a straightjacket, an excuse not to live according to what we think. Of course, it's easy for me to say, I have a century of sufficiency between my breast and my back.

I am not an enigmatic woman, I am not the Gioconda, not your tropical Gypsy, not one of Rafael's Madonna's. You should have painted a different portrait. You rendered me quiet, forever stopped in time. And the worst thing is that people keep passing in front of me. They speak indifferently. Despite the watchman asking for silence, they keep talking about this and that, a soldier adjusts his pistol, a

boyfriend clutches his girlfriend's breast...my lips contract with envy, but no one notices.

That girl might not return home tonight, like me who told a lie and didn't return. They looked for me like crazy, my mother managed to preserve her authority: "I told you so, I told you, the dead little fly... then she'll be scared, I forgive you everything...!" Was that all? "As long as she comes back..." Because if I went out into the world, if I went into the world, she also lost. The chorus of neighbors encouraged her: "You'll see, it will all end well." My mother wails, she moves once more before me, I've been hiding behind the warehouse walls, outside my routine, outside...even outside the world for a few hours. But, cowardly as always, I reappear. I see my mother's skirt in the night wind, I see her desolation. "Mother, I love you so, here I am...."

I go out, like I want to leave this frame right now, this prison, but everything changed. I've offended her and she yells: "Whore, such a crazy daughter, what kind of game are you playing, straying so far from your own...?" My mother cries and all those who look for my silhouette leave.

I am neither dead nor alive. You are to blame for this image that neither breathes nor exists. I dreamt I had lost myself, dreamt I walked the world alone, and I am nailed here. What will they be afraid if I exchange this look for a look of hunger? To be hungry and look at the sea like those in this port, hunger to see other skies.

I am moving toward the infinite, inside myself. Right now. I churn up my life's insignificance, I look for a pearl, I am afraid of losing myself among so many days that are the same. I would like to crash...search, find, destroy, my hands breaking open shells so some light will come from them. Perhaps I will find some family treasure to calm my misery, why not. A pretty uniform button my grandmother kept from her husband who died for his country. Is it a family relic? She grew old and silent hiding that button, behind a silent door.

You saved me from that, from growing old. Although, like her, I have memories. Half my memories are useless, they serve only for intensifying what no longer exists: inconformity. Or to look at what

wasn't a real path, but random, sometimes going forward, sometimes back, and that makes a life of all the time contained in your head.

No, no, although motionless I am not dry, I can still dream. No one can take my dreams from me. Or can they? To dream...isn't that also to live?

Who do I ask? Do they have the right to tell us which dreams are possible and which aren't? This place is a point of confluences. A port. Some go off alone and leave promising they will return; others go and already know it is goodbye forever; others sit on the wall to look at the horizon, asking the sea when, when will you change my life, why is the piece of sea that separates us from the world like an open window through which we say goodbye and receive and wait.

Ah, if we spoke only what is necessary...I speak to myself and to you, you who again and again return from your horrible death, in nightmares, the death of a wounded animal, one who suffers.

Look at this face, look well at what you have never seen. I have never been satisfied. I have done nothing, only dreamed gratuitously. I wanted another life and you, who had the opportunity to give it to me, did nothing. And they said you were transgressive... Not with me, with me you were the gentleman, the cocky lad... "Come on, Dolly, fasten my boots and walk with me through the port."

The birds, when night comes, cannot be seen in the sky. And he looked for them so he might fire at them with the tip of his walking stick and was on fire: I wanted heat, but he walked as if he were with a saint. Again and again like that.

Marcela López Gravina

I Have Lied, Given Birth, and Loved

A Woman

Did you see that my lips are pressed shut now, J? I know I am still hanging above your bed and you've often commented on my birds, my breasts and my straps. They are just some of my amulets, my makeup. Small tricks, or however you prefer to call them. What time is it in Santiago? Are those mountains still there?

The picture you are looking at is an old photograph. If it's not an oval portrait today, it was at one time: back then I looked straight at you. I have lied to you so often.... I should tell you that I am also not called Julia, nor is it true that I come from the sea. Although you have sometimes licked my salty mermaid's tail or pulled off a scale which I have set aflame for you to use in a line of poetry. Although you remember sliding down my mercury eyes to ocean depths where you remained without air and at my mercy, I didn't come from the sea. I confess.

My name is Ana, I was born in a forest and this is the moment of my perfection, that's why I am not looking at you. I asked the painter for a few things. The first: that the tangle of my hair would be visible, I didn't want you to wake up one day and hear from others that I'd committed the crime without telling you. You, so far away, dazzled by the color of my nipples without ever having suspected. It wouldn't have been fair. The second: that you leave me bound to those small wings forever, although they're useless for flying, they cover my back with feathers and protect the dragons that, although they also have wings, I have tattooed using needles on my flesh. I have no clothing because at my age it's time to begin to walk naked. Are you going to tell me that the picture's background is black? I know. Nevertheless, I haven't needed pills, nor specialists for my existence. But all these

are unimportant details, you yourself can look for them, or continue to invent them, like you've done with me ever since you hung that damned picture on your bedroom wall.

I think that I have lied, given birth and loved

Tonight I am crying at the foot of my sister's bed. Her body bears my pain. I plan a murder capable of relieving us, and I am impotent: I drink from her morphine drip, inject myself with her needle, swallow and drown with her damaged throat. I need someone to help me. I watch her sleep and moan. I look at her hair hung over the fan. I am going to tighten the straps across my arms and breasts until they hurt. My head explodes with hurt birds, blue and violet. The word no longer exists, the floor is covered with blood, no grimace comes as I swallow the most horrible scream. These useless fingers remain, putting out their nets. Threads that go on like sticky tousled letters. The night, the little drops, the wait.

I am going to invent a prayer: *Birds that nested in me, do not abandon me, sink your beaks into me to the end.*

Wake up.

A bird from the forest

It is dawn and it's not Havana. I turn the television on and see the man in the red sweater climbing a hill made of sand in a forest I know. The cameras, the reporters, the technical police are all following him. He has the face of a tired wolf. Where did his brilliant mind remain on the morning of the crime? I go back over every letter of his messages to find it: "you will love me because I am weak, shameless and useless...don't give up...my duty is to play you fair...if I hadn't said something you wouldn't have noticed anything strange...." It might have been perfect, but numbers have never trapped me. I always invent the words. His writing smelled of that substance I shouldn't mention just now, only the bait attracts me. I managed to see him in photographs wearing a tie, standing beside the president, with a strange

optimistic smile, with a small earring in his ear like the one in the painter's portraits. I didn't know Cioran, and was confused.

Three times he left me waiting and failed to come. The feathers of his coat smelling of cinnamon, his painted nails, the birds in his hair brushed out so he wouldn't notice my inventions at first. He didn't come. His last message said: "Forgive me, a friend died in an accident, I am devastated." Even my children laughed at me as I undressed, cursing. I tightened the leather straps I have on my arms and flapped around the room filling it with perfume and wind. The next thing I did was delete him from my contacts, believing that an optimistic mathematician, although he wrote music or delirious messages, would be unable to gallop on birds. I didn't hear anything more from you until the morning of the crime.

Now I know I was guilty. On the tele they say you were behind it all, that the noose you used was found in your house, that there was no hooded man behind the tree, and no one was following you but you, Little Red Riding Hood. I who imagined you surrounded by music and wine that stormy night of my menstruation, see you for the first time now as a human animal in the police reports of the morning news. You carry the pain, or shame, hanging like remnants in your neck scarf before the cameras: you have your black beard and the little earring, in your ear, is like an anchor from the past.

"Now I can love you,"—I send a message to your cell phone. I suppose you won't answer while you are under arrest. Then I run and ask the painter to urgently add something to my portrait: a space where a naked man isn't alone and can hold onto a bird and not fall. The strap that so skillfully appears was also mine. It's the one I use to bind my arms and wings. It's clear they wanted to kill you, you didn't lie. You don't justify yourself or cry.

When I leave the portrait, and attach my mermaid's tail, I will hide the mountain birds

The greatest party I know is my own. Nothing keeps me from inventing it all over again and returning to the sea. I am like a warm-

blooded amphibian with gills that softly allow your names to come and go. On summer nights, I tend to lurk about the island that once offered me certain secrets. I was once a woman, and on solid ground gave savage birth to two sons. Howling like a she-wolf, crying like a flower, I was born immortal that day: cave being, granddaughter of a galaxy, daughter of rough weather. I understood that the mountain, or the gods, were mine. And that I could never fail to tend my animal. If I had not loosened my entrails upon the earth I would have had to silence half my words, but I did. Now I bear deep scars and have four mermaid tails, I believe they belong to me and that's where the eternal party is. I always look for the man who knows how to dance like I dance, and offer him my infinite rain of scales. If I have been enchanting it's only because cold frightens me, and I want an entire forest to protect me. I have given everything. I have looked at you. I do not cut my hair nor is it possible for me to forget you. Look for me if you can, I will give you this delight. I have already begun to comb the wings I will use tomorrow. My one condition is that you arrive naked.

Vertigo occurs at the beginning and end

I wasn't interested in posing for the painter. I preferred to tattoo his drawings on my thighs, but that wasn't possible. This afternoon I walked the whole neighborhood of Alamar, beneath an October sun, looking for ink and needles that never appeared. In that search, the road and those who accompanied me led me without wanting to the place where I always end up.

Since childhood I have seen everything from this place. Women who were very white and drunk, their bodies covered with bruises, emerged from the foam in winter having fun with their lovers. Little Portuguese boats with long blue and violet threads they could tangle like the birds. Fishermen scraping the scales from fish with their knives. Lonely guys masturbating in their eternal raca-raca. Black police in blue uniforms, bottles with messages, dusks, dawns, rains. I have been all of this.

I like this place since the Russians were here, it was never really a beach. It has sharpened Dog Teeth, waves that knock you over and sea urchins with black spikes. I learned to swim here, I must have been eight years old. One morning, back then, I walked with my grandfather Alfredo through the puddles that form on the rocks, and felt like the sea was drinking me. The foam sucked one leg. That was when I learned about vertigo. My grandfather said it was a little octopus that had gotten hold of me and I didn't want to look, I knew for sure it was the depths and the foam. I don't remember much, just that something traps you unexpectedly and your life goes back to the beginning.

Today we find neither ink nor tattoo artist. My grandfather lies dead in another city. I came here by a different path. I wanted to see the house that was mine when I was a child and I asked a friend to come along. We drank beer. When we approached, I saw that everything was in its place except us.

In front of the house was the thicket where I played, now they raise goats and pigs there. At three in the afternoon, when the sun pounds your head, there is no one in those places. We crossed, I had to urinate on the ground. I raised my dress, crouched down and wet the cracked earth. Smoke rose, the goats and he looked at me with warm eyes I've tried to retain.

We didn't speak again, we walked looking for the sea. He hummed songs until I mentioned my grandfather, the octopus and the foam of that place. We got to the shore walking on the Dog Teeth. There the water broke against the rocks. I bent down at the place I thought I remembered and he said: "I have to urinate here, on your hands, between you and the waves." He did so marvelously, with a small rainbow behind his stream, an enormous rainbow. I held out my hands so all the rains would soak them and felt the foam swallowing me and it was a party that went on forever. We squeezed our wet hands, greeted the masturbator, the fisherman, the policeman...we vowed never to see each other again. What kind of a pact was that?

Then I ran to the painter's house and told him: "Make my portrait

here, before it gets dark. Close my mouth and open some birds." I cannot continue to speak. It may be that so many nests weigh down the body, but I remember all the colors that were mine. I am here.

<div style="text-align: right">

Montevideo, September 2009
Inspired by the works of the painter Roberto Fabelo.

</div>

Lizabel Mónica

Exercising the Productive "Einbildungskraft" Dramatic Game with Hannah

—Hello.
—Hello, John—said Yahíma.
—Hello—said Z.
—Is this table all right?
—Fine—said John.
—Yes, just fine—said Yahíma.

First Act

Action without a name, a "who" attached to it, is meaningless.
—Hannah Arendt

Hannah I. Who am I? My name is Hannah. I am Jewish. But it's not about what, but who. It's not about my qualities, my talents or defects. It's about my life. I have thought, I have loved, I...have judged. I am seventy-one now. We are in 1975. The century is young and old, like me. Along its furrows, in contrast to my own, its makes itself up to look younger.

Fresh blood runs through its veins; tired blood through mine.

This is the best moment to ask me who I am. I mean, I know I have acted. I took the stage. I played my part. I did so avoiding authorial pretension. I *went astutely toward the unknown.*

I was action.

But my steps are getting shorter. These ribs bear the weight of a life. I have given everything in front of the chorus. Today I want to know: has my life finally been an event?

Hannah II. Isn't this too theatrical? The spirit of tragedy shouldn't replace, but rather embody, the spirit of the life. Why are you laughing?

Hannah III. It's Eichmann; it's...incredibly evil and incredibly ridiculous. Why are you fleeing?

Hannah IV. The drama is really nothing but an imitation of the action.

Hannah V. Is writing action?

Hannah VI. To submit your opinion to the public, that's action.

Hannah VII. You can keep on laughing and laughing hard. What do you want? I am Hannah *the disagreeable*. Isn't that what they always called me?

Hannah VIII. It doesn't matter. The question of "who" is part of the action, and the action demands narration.
 What they said doesn't matter. They cannot judge.
 Analysis only comes after the fact. In front of the audience.

Second Act

He performed in the marketplace the way the flute-player
performed at a banquet. It is sheer performance, sheer activity.
 —Hannah Arendt, On Socrates

CHORUS. January, 1940. Hannah Arendt and Heinrich Blücher were married in France.
 A few months later, Hannah was summoned to Vel d'Hiv, and then transported to the camp at Gurs. That summer Hannah, like many others, escaped. She went to her friends at Montauban. There, when she thought they might not see each other again, she and her husband found one another. They left for New York.

In 1942, a year after her arrival in North America, they heard about the extermination camps, and of the transfer to Auschwitz of those imprisoned at Gurs. From that moment on, and forever, Hannah was a survivor.

Woman I. No life, whatever it is, can do without a narrator, or a poet, or a historian. Without her, all one has done remains futile. The poet has the talent to write the story. She alone has that talent. The poet, the *pariah*, the *schlemihl*, the unfortunate and disgraced one. Yes, all those Yiddish words... The Greek tradition holds vision, gaze, light. The Jewish tradition holds the voice and the word.

Woman II. The *Sabbath Princess*, the public voice, the voice of the plaza.

Woman III. The poet Heine, he who stopped being the voice of man to become the Chorus in Greek plays; Heine, the shadow and the dog.

Woman IV. Enough. These are simply truths. And I have pronounced too many.

Woman V. Definitely. Who am I to doubt so little?

Woman VI. I am the woman. I am all human beings. I am a single human. I am all Women, all Men. I am a Jew.

Woman VII. I have completed the first two chapters of the book I've loved best, the book I consider necessary. Yet I am afraid to continue.

Woman VIII. I know what I am not, and knowing what I am is denied me. What I Represent.

Woman IX. Dante said it: *In every act the first intention of the protagonist is to reveal his own image.*

Woman X. But this is impossible. In the action each of us is, in the dual meaning of the word, both agent and patient. We are subjects of our own history.

Woman XI. We need to get to the end of the act, to access the event.

Between Acts

—Good whisky—said Yahíma.

—Yes—said John.

—Let's drink to Hannah—said Z.

—We can't just say: *To Hannah.*

—No, you're right, that won't work.

—I know—said Z—To Karla.

They raise their mugs.

—To Karla!

—I ask myself what they would be doing now.

—Probably sitting on top of Mount Everest, drinking beer with Harold Pinter.

—And who is Karla?

—One of Karl Marx's alter egos. A character. I just invented her. She is vulgar, totally unconcerned with intellect. Not unconcerned, let's just say unaware.

—Completely the opposite of Hannah.

—What is *a different woman?*

—You know, those women who surpass the stereotype. One who can sit and talk with the playwright or write the play herself.

—Little women-playwrights?

—Yes, in a way. Beneath, giving birth.

—What do you think Hannah would say?

—She would say: The difference between the sexes is diversity—said Z.

—Do you know the point? Do you know what it is?

—What.

—Politics are based on the fact of man's plurality.

—And of woman's—said Yahíma.

—Politics is about being together, with others, but different. Being together while being different.

—Of course, the *polis*—said John.

—Yes, the *polis*.

—I'm beginning to see it. Karla is a comic character, isn't she?—said Yahíma.

—What I'm trying to say is that Hannah was clear on this point.

The difference between the sexes is diversity. God created the human being. Genesis (1:27): *He created them man and woman.* But itinerant Saint Paul, anxious for salvation, confuses the syntax, forces the relationship: woman was created *from* man and *for* man.

—Saint Paul is an example of...*a man*, who separates himself from...*the political*—said John.

—In all his writings, fear of difference stands out, here and there all the time he confuses diversity with otherness, he transfigures the only diverse people into many peoples who are enemies: other people set traps wherever you look, even within themselves.... Saint Paul exercises terror rather than power.

—A government of domination, not concertation.

—Do you know that joke about Lenin...? Lenin is speaking to the Russian people: "Capitalism is man's exploitation of man...."

—As far as I'm concerned, to be a woman among men is to be plural.

—The idea the contemporary world has of politics...—John begins to say.

—And then he said: "So you'll see, comrades, socialism is just the opposite!"

Third Act

I am convinced that understanding is closely related to
that faculty of imagination which Kant called Einbildungskraft
and which has nothing in common with fictional ability.
 —Hannah Arendt

Jewish Woman I. Let no one write about me like I wrote about Rahel.

Jewish Woman II. Furthermore, how to avoid the birth of truths.

Jewish Woman III. I tried to tell her life as and how she might have done it herself.

Jewish Woman IV. Maybe I shouldn't finish the book.

Jewish Woman V. But my dear Karl Jaspers found it too critical a biography, sometimes ruthless.

Jewish Woman VI. Perhaps it would be worthwhile to indicate its unfinished nature, more than its ideas.

Jewish Woman VII. I am only now thinking clearly about it. Underline what is unfinished. Suggest and cut.

Jewish Woman VIII. The I, said the good Nietzsche, can only be known in life in an exalted state that borders on drunkenness.

Jewish Woman IX. I never reigned myself in, I was always imprudent, I followed my judgement to the end. I was probably right, more so than I thought, when I wrote the last sentence in my book about Isak Dinesen: *Wisdom belongs to the third stage of life and it seems it only comes to those who, in their youth, were neither wise nor prudent.*

Jewish Woman X. But if we don't judge that way, if we don't judge with all the vitality of the spirit, I don't know how we judge.

Jewish Woman XI. Might nearness to death not be a drunken state?

Between Acts

—I am thinking rather of a theater piece. Couldn't you produce a dramatic work?—said Z.

—Theater? You mean a play?—said John.

—The thing is, for Hannah theater is, was, the best sort of politics. She said nowhere else is the political sphere of human life transposed in art as it is there.

—She said that? No, no I cannot produce theater.

—Let's make a movie.

—A movie.

—Yes, that's what we'll do.

Last Act

I would have confronted the alternative: to write or not to write. Because one can also hold one's tongue.
 —Hannah Arendt, in conversation with Günter Gaus

Chorus. 1975: *there is always a before and after. In "the before," you simply write, speak, discuss in front of a bored and expectant audience. In "the after" you die. Once dead, your word passes into other hands, that will rewrite it again and again, producing new works. Your work will only be finished by those, who read between teeth, who ponder your words, who can address you for the first time. Your readers. Those who will know who you were, who you are... In this act, you have no voice.*

Here is the border. In these days of 1975, where death prowls clandes-

tinely and then at last visits, Hannah Arendt is at home, seated at her desk. Staring fixedly at the typewriter. She is trying to work on the last chapter of her book Life of the Mind. *The first two parts are done:* Thinking *and* Willing. *It's* Judging's *turn. Hannah hesitates, her fingers tremble on those keys to which she is so accustomed. When they find her dead, sometime after the moment just described, there is only a sheet of paper in the machine, barely begun.*

Basilia Paspatamatíu

Bad Memory

I

When did I meet Esteban?

I forget more than I remember My damaged mind prevents
sufficient lucidity Must I resign myself? Resign myself and sigh?
Sigh and desire? Just thinking about what I've lost whole frag-
ments of my life I will not retrieve as dead as I am soon enough
 When did I meet him?
 I need to recuperate the dreams where I enthroned him

 Esteban philosopher? Marksman? Asthmatic? Beloved baby?
 cruel child who killed frogs? The only boy who showed his penis?
 do you remember that and me?
 or the one who shouted more than the others? and who later
soon after became my idol my impossible love my model to follow

 But did I really know him? What was he like? I need to
know I have his portrait
 was he like that?

 I am called Julia and I will always wait for him

II

 I was alone and vulnerable in a world of dogmas and rules
those from above and those from below those wanted and those
not those that think for you masculine pleasures and permanent
harassment honor was lost and blood ran asphyxiated subdued

brothers humiliated and blamed you they sacrificed you and fled
because you were the bad one

But Esteban freed me I should be grateful to him shouldn't
I?

From then on, we were the protagonists in an extraordinary his-
tory as if we were predestined in deep communion in a pact of
silence a hidden alliance Situated in another dimension we
knew we were invisible untouchable unpunished beyond borders
out of reach with incomparable plenty And more intensely alive
the closer we were to death And for the noblest reasons on earth
A closely guarded secret Will we know what it is one day?

The world was a theater of operations for us And we were the
only people in the play Heroes and saints at the same time Or
avenging angels in an evil universe without redemption? And
although audience and applause were missing it was an event that
made us feel free and happy
 We possessed the passion of vertigo the mystique of giving our-
selves to a powerful attraction of the risk the greater the risk the
greater the glory The lie was our weapon and love our rebellion
violence a routine
 And a lot of fear of not being able of not being of service of
making a mistake becoming cowards fear of betrayal of infidelity of
blindness of intolerance of fanaticism of pain of injustice the injustice
of pain
 Were we the nation's best children?

III

*Identify ourselves with the other think and alienate ourselves for
the other exercise and execute accept the decisions look for the goal
without disorder no chaos complete the plan don't share or commu-*

nicate go on alone don't ask for help don't denounce yourself we can't trust nor wait for anyone always on the move don't lose your way one distraction can be fatal look both ways don't rush into it avoid being followed don't forget but don't forgive either don't let yourself be swayed don't forget to calculate to plan come and go promptly don't wait don't linger continue the march always advance advance look for a solution without doubting without stopping or going back a ref-uge at least don't let yourself be trapped if there is no salvation make yourself small disguise yourself change your shirt your hair your voice your way of walking the disguise will save you soil yourself bury yourself in stench wrapped as if in a shroud resist to the death I know you can no one like you no one better than you (Esteban's words)

In silence and in shadow On a trip without return?

We glided carefully above the interminable abyss that stretched out beneath our feet as they skimmed along their crazy journey because of the tenacious persecution excited by the great danger until fearlessly launching ourselves and then breaking apart against that giant unbridgeable wall inevitably rising before us covering and darkening the entire horizon

It was a question of life or death

We were on a mission

IV

We are alone now lost on this desert without breath and without strength without any protection or help no more illusions or prospects no future goals or renewed hope (no papas or mamas or children with whom to play no fresh flowers or fruit or music or dances or perfumes or wreathes or bright lights or colored pencils or trees to climb or desire to run or to live)

To pray in vain to curse in vain?

Is this the end? a horrible defeat?

Listen to the roar of the weapons feel the stench of fallen bod-
ies observe the smoke the powder gives off the screams of terror
and aid the flutter of birds so many fallen after such a dramatic
wait before such impetuous ferocity so much extreme cruelty the
expected retaliation by those who had never expected this possibility
this luck not even when they laughed frivolously as they held to the
slightest glimmer of the most remote signal if they kill them it's for
a reason it's for a reason

 Alone and surrounded by land and water land and water we
will always be hungry and thirsty but all we ask for is a little peace
so we can replace and repair and we only hope resting softly barely
opening our serene eyes ready to dream only wanting to sleep
and dream
 Rescue impossible Must I resign myself? Or insist until
exhausted
 Fade and wake
 Wake and resist Again Again and again Forever

V

 Are we the losers? do they want us vanquished? must we accept
with resignation? Will the world one day learn our well-kept
secret? How do we continue existing without losing without allowing
ourselves to be overcome without discarding or forgetting what we did
for so many years with so much weariness so many agonies so much
faith courage and passion accompanied only by the greatest amount of
guilt the most debilitating thoughts and our profound affliction from
so many images and so many lost words

 But time doesn't pass in vain we diminish more all the time
weakened smaller less stable mere thread of a voice glassy eyes fragile
transparent skin dry mouth trembling limbs shivering beneath a men-
acing sky on this long cold night

Like true human leftovers and soon enough simply powdery
vestiges that air and wind will finally dissolve and disperse
 Irreparable pathway to decline and extinction?

 Could we have once imagined that this would be our end? And
did Esteban suspect it did he foresee it? Did I really know Esteban?
Does he still expect something of me?

 Is it a field of flowers? His flowering majesty,
 flowers for his majesty.
 And his court, the beautiful courtesans, so light,
 so rosy, so flirtatious,
 so regal. All flowers. And the sea in the background,
 and the blue sky behind...

But it is only a bad painting that masks something that hides
 what I must find and our salvation depends on it
 The only way out when by then all the other doors have
 closed

 Julia

 To D., my friend in Paris, disappeared in Buenos Aires

Reina María Rodríguez

Aurora Borealis

The more we esteem material goods,
the more easily we give and receive,
and the less grateful we are for them.
 —Marina Tsvetáyeva

We continue going up and down to the Kremlin
(its tower looks like a toy)
and Asia wants to take her sled
for Three Kings Day—like me, looking in store windows—,
for woolen clothes as gifts
breads to give others for Christmas
even aware, as she was, that bread
doesn't deserve any gratitude.
But everything stays open and empty
almost no one there
no exchanges.

"The sled is from Asia"
and Marina comes wearing a tiger skin
Mandalstam calls "a leopard".
On the sled we also ride with María
who just gave birth to a baby girl
(his first granddaughter).
Lía will be her name.
"From my ring finger to your pinky"—he told me.

And I put on the cat stone,
its pretty little silver face
protecting me from the storm

—he is also newborn—
like a little girl or small animal who will arrive despite the knots
on this island of sugar that isn't snow,
but will pretend it is and grow
in winter along the coast
like I once pretended to be the aurora borealis
on his eyelids.

I don't know why you let a snowstorm be the cause
and also the consequence of loss!
I have no sister
—nor a pearly white tooth sharpened to mark
a territory to which I can retreat
when the sled crashes and overturns
and demolishes us more than how we already are!
When I tell you it isn't the Kremlin we see
nor will my granddaughter be yours.
That in my delirium,
I will know it is not Marina with Asia adjusting
those skins to the contours of a map
or to a labyrinth we come to.

Another fraud, to say that at Christmas we are family
when we bring a gift without a tiger without skins or sled:
an embrace from Mandelstam:
a sacrificed leopard he stole
for his neck.

Only a poor vagabond cat on my finger
signals how he hides
his loneliness
and knows how to lick
without being a leopard.

Ah, Marina, your day!

"I saw the wood"
—you light the stove—
"...I wash the potatoes in freezing water
I later boil in the samovar."
It is all old: the samovar, the potatoes, the day.
The stove with its lit coals
the dress with its brown skirt
—always the same—
I sleep in it too.
The bucket, I ask myself: will there be a prayer to the bucket?
when you make one you will understand
the bucket is the heart of the house
where the stove, the samovar
and the little girl's brown-gray eyes
are revealed.
"One could not live without the bucket."

Puddles everywhere, sighs
"a desperate desire the floor be clean!"
And shine.
The water is also on loan
—the misery no.
A neighbor gives me matches, bread, sawdust...
The utensils too are from someone else
(we receive and separate ourselves from them
with neither pain nor confidence).
"The bathroom key hanging from my neck"
is neither crucifix nor pearl
doesn't open any entrance
but that one, to the children's garden
where they give out the supplementary ration
and "not a single free finger" remains.

On my return, I untie the little girl,
she just ate
half a raw cabbage
and passed out
tied to the little chair
then
I write, smoke and write
what is left.

All that is left...
Very late at night I cut wood for the following day.

Ah, Marina, the Night!

...I didn't want to tell more than my day.

By rope I climb to the loft
without a ladder
(the ladder burned)
and go down again looking for a book
—the floor is cold, frozen and burns
the soles of my feet.
I go through "seven closed doors"
The bell disappeared
"it doesn't work since the beginning of the revolution."
Useless as it was, someone stole it.
There's a knocker now,
but no one arrives
nor does anyone ask for Marina:
"Marina, daughter, "where are you hiding?"
Alia and I go down in the dark
(the bannister also burned)
and we no longer hold on
we fly attached

to the bannister's murmur
floating in our ears
—has the wind moved it—
the bannister?
the little girl?

But perhaps we never go down
and always remain in the dark
with the letters of a prayer
—soup—
in the knots of rope
(of broth)
with which I hang myself each night
like one more potato.

"In general, the notion is round."
"Embodiment, sharp"
he explained to her.
But Alia understands neither notion nor embodiment
brings us down from the loft
to where Goethe is
playing around in the cellar,
reading out loud
when the knocker sounds
and I enter.

Soleida Ríos and Jamila M. Ríos

Focus on a Point in the Back and Speak

I

I'm one of those who arrives at the podium early. (Did I park where I should have beneath the jagüey tree?) I brush from the table the bits of chalk from Friday's event. Is everyone there now? I overcome the knot in my stomach and face them. I put on a smile and project my voice: Good morning... I look down at the table again and organize my two bags. One of books, the other my handbag. In the second: my house and car keys, coin purse, telephone, glasses, sunglasses, identity cards, two fountain pens, a couple of photos of La Niña, one old coin, a plastic bag in case I want to bring home some boring pastry from the cafeteria. In the first: the Bible—the Mexican version of that theoretical work—, Aristotle's Poetics, Plato's *Kratylos* and an extra watch.

I remove that watch and place it on the table, subtly, on the cleanest part. (Will they take note of the gesture? Will they finally quiet down?) I look at the watch on my wrist. Almost eight... Shall we begin? I ask the question politely, hoping the murmuring will subside, that they will settle in their places, stop moving the desks, begin to open their notebooks and then—*Mon Dieu*—their minds...

I go over to the door and close it. Let anyone wanting to come in do so during the second act. I smile and sit down. (How hot it is!) Good morning, to those I haven't greeted yet.... The lights blink. (One-two-three, one-two-three.) I recognize the rhythm right away. I take a deep breath and let it out quietly so they won't notice my nerves, that even my toes are sweating. With more confidence I open my fan, like someone parting the curtains when she gets home so the fresh air will enter, like someone opening the theater curtain while the others

spin. Although if it was winter I would feel comfortable enough: a hand-embroidered shawl around my shoulders.

(Let's see, my dear, focus on a point in the back and speak. Concentrate and try to put yourself at ease with a saving *pas de deux*. Where should I begin? With the same good girls as always? Of whom should I ask a question? That fish over there, with glassy eyes, her scales hidden behind her book? Have they spent the weekend reading or have they danced the nights away in their enviable times at the casino, later falling exhausted into bed?)

Let's begin with love. In the end, every good read (laying on the wedding bed, mouth in open admiration at the lectern, pads of your fingers moistened to help you move from page to page) is, first and foremost, about pleasure...a never-ending conversation between two people, a convulsive act of love, that begins to subside as we accommodate our enthusiasm to that which attracts us, until it has us writing the questions that occur to us and our silent sighs in the book's margins. Hand in hand with Plato (disguised as Socrates), with his theory of asexuality, his half orange, I make my *entrée*. Later I can talk to them about the origins of languages and the eternal dispute between the natural and the arbitrary. Later I can tell them truth doesn't hide, even in the runaway verb. But first I want to talk to them about love. Like any good sophist, I go from the known to the unknown. It's the adagio, the slow movement, and with it the most famous couples I can remember: Romeo and Juliet, Don Quijote and Dulcinea, Giselle and Albrecht, Tristan and Isolde, Dianan and Acteon.... They, we, take our *promenades*. I play at standing on my toe on only one leg, as Plato (or was it Socrates?), gallant as he is, holds me by the hand and then around the waist, and parades, blue tail, Argos' hundred eyes (demanding and solicitous) about me.

Ufff...I haven't danced for a long time, but am so enthused by the essay's *leit-motif* as a sexual act, by writing about the other as mirror and commentary, as dancing speculation, as mating dance...that I cannot abandon it. I ride one digression after another and then another, until I finally arrive at the heart of the matter. Even more, once I hit my stride I become adventurous, take risks, am determined to go on....

I breathe. I open, close, agitate the fan. I wanted to talk to them about women's writing by taking the hand of Hélène Cixous (disguised as Clarice Lispector), Virginia Woolf (wearing Dulce María Loynaz's cape)...I wanted to talk to them about para-literature, the sub-genres, letters, diaries, testimony hand in hand with Elizabeth Burgos (under/upon Rigoberta Menchú's tongue)...I wanted to speak to them of autobiography. About books by women who traveled the Caribbean, my Humboldt Street. I don't know if it's the *Aguas primaverales* or the masquerade ball of *El carnival de Venecia*, but I feel especially confessional today. Concentrate, my father would say, as he pushed the small bicycle. Look at the screen, Lisandro would say, as he tried to watch his favorite program and I just talked and talked, chattering, spewing, speechifying, as I pumped the pedals hard as I could....

I wanted to devour the world, encapsulate it with the stroke of a pen and place it at their feet. Make it bloom in their sleepyheads. But I cannot give them everything. And you must see to believe. I sigh. Well, let's pick up where we left off last week....

When I look up again, the first act is over. (Have I said half of what I had to say?) Are they bored? Come what may, I never question those long faces, don't allow myself to be trapped, even if they tied me down, by their floating fish eyes. I settle on an amiable look or, in lieu of real connection, a point in the back; and continue to weave my interest in the fixed word, the written letter, a terrain upon which it is necessary to dig with an archeologist's pick, always finding something new: ever deeper, as if descending with Orpheus into the regions of hell, searching for the beloved, like one going down to drink the blood of the dead, to become ever wiser and ask the questions that will save him from his own Odyssey.

Okay, where were my arrows landing? I ask casually, until someone picks up the thread and, with the ability of a trained athlete, I lean over the table once again. I put my hands together and clap rhythmically to see if that will help me sustain my rush of *words, words, words*.... The drums might also be a ring, a sign of fire to be leapt across, feet in a scissors kick. I feel my body, like when I first learned to ride a bike, pushed by my father's hands along Misiones Avenue. I see

the whole landscape at first and then only the street: almost endless, opening before me like a path fashioned of pure will, from which I will emerge victorious. Let Aristotle and Barthes, Foucault and Homi Bhabha, Derridá and bell hooks accompany me. With them I make a parade of the most picturesque folk I know for the final act: not two by two, nor one-two-three, but four by four, a march of the masses, parade of feet.

Where was I? Like the cat chasing the ball, where is the yarn's end leading into the mouse's cave? My feet sweat. I remove my shoes and they fly through the air. I look down at the professorial table, shielded now. Plato, Aristotle, the masters of rhetoric, French philosophers, feminists, divine communion with its jaws wide open, like dreamt beasts, I must cross a bridge, a great bridge, a tightrope, the highway to Guanajay on my little bicycle, peddling as hard as I can.... They look at me with open mouths, waiting to see how I'll get out of this one, waiting to see if I slip and fall. But they don't know that each time I stray from the road I plant a tree, that each digression is another card I pull from my sleeve, a display of crystal, a rainbow, a bit of red coral I sow, a bouquet of jet against the evil spirits.

This is the hour of the pirouettes, I say, gathering my full skirt and spinning, spinning perfectly balanced on one foot. The Girl flies with me, or is it that attentive face to my left, or is it that dazed seal who comes from her stupor and jumps like a flying fish? I woke them with my drumming, *Mon Dieu*, I cannot believe it. Now everyone is looking at the blackboard, everyone is attentive to the table, waiting for the great leap, the string of mounting associations that will come from my mouth and take me to heaven, take me away from here.... Like a cat climbing higher and higher, and then meows in fear wanting to come back down. I feel faint. I no longer know who leads who. But the Girl propels me, like when we danced together to popular songs on the radio, like when we would go to the park and I would push her on the swing, on the merry-go-round: like when we went swimming and brushed the bottom sand and came up holding hands, until we were on the surface again, our faces turned toward the sun.... You must know how to swim, you must know how to dance, you must

know how to give yourself to the bicycle of life. It's all a question of legs and arms, a question of throwing your body into the fight. Am I falling now, or am I fading at last, tired of this discourse, this song, split from endless rumor. Everyone approaches. Everyone looks. My feet are bare, freed from the slavery of the last. It doesn't matter if they are a bit aged, if they carry the marks of the pedals and of sea urchins, of ballet slippers and the stones I walked on along the Maya Riviera, the Great Wall of China, among the pointed cupulas of Moscow...I spin and they carry me up to where I touch the ceiling, higher than the beams. Curious perch. I am raised like the figurehead on the boat's prow, I am headed out to the sea above which I hovered, measuring my comings and goings, the notes in my book. I have taught those I love almost all I knew. I have covered them with my Verb, like a mother in the night, like the loving wife, up to their necks, their noses, I have placed my creed in their mouths like a spoonful of honey. Upon their morning pillows I also scattered the dust of my wings, it always remains between my fingers, like a perfume that escapes, like the edges of an album studied to the end.

II

Like Isadora, I could dance that armchair. I dance the casino wheel, I dance my bicycle's wheel...Heian...Heian...Heian.... My body dances here, it sways on the Operating Table:

Curtains (blinds...?) lightbulbs, formaldehyde, scissors, forceps, needles, scalpel...
sylphs and swans, peasants and Spaniards, maidens and slaves, madwomen and dolls, princesses and queens; waltzes, polkas, gavottes and tarantellas, immobilized dancing figures.... Anesthetized.

But the swan...the black swan. Pride, elegance, seduction... Standing tall, the crown on its head. The stage, the world...Four *pirouettes* in the fourth position/ four *fouetté*...Abrupt, the free leg

inscribing a circle...and, with impetus, concluding: five *pirouettes* bring the audience to its feet, all together, as one, feverish, shouting, jumping on the seats.

Bravo! Powwwerfullll!!! Bravoooooooo!!!

And the operating room... Lights, more lights, all the lights. Waves of Tchaikovsky. Momento: clean cut, round; the perfect slaughter house. Sliced, amputated, dismembered, the swan's glorious wing... destroyed now, useless, from one cold blow, to the cold tray, the muddy water of investigation.

She narrates.

Hidden or far off place, a river, a door in the mountain.... Also in the nation.

One sign and another: Here (Antilles, archipelago), In Japan, in Russia, between Nepal and Tibet, in Korea...

Is the name an omen?

The names speak, the body speaks, your hands speak...in Bustamante's hands (mudras). Water from the rock: four drops four times a day. Beech: "I make peace with myself." This mouth will speak twenty times, twenty times four times a day, these same words: "I am in my neighbor, my neighbor is in me."

And Growth will have to be recognized, even in such a confusing pact with *Error*? Error of the body. The *nest*, that *nest* (right-handed), adding and subtracting without discarding, creating real discord, abnormal embodiment of a mental recourse?

Can the mind, deformed or eaten away like that, make way for deep and intangible wounds, for sustained resentment, for a false belief in the uselessness of everything...can the mind become an agent of restoration?

Four drops, four times a day. Under the tongue. We must rethink such a brief and difficult poem "Coarse mane." Knife...thread of blood: *Only love engenders...only Love.* But the body...

Speaking of the body: 31 underarm lymph nodes (on the right side), all of them clean; bones and fleshy parts, clean. Clean. *Errorless.* This laughter, you know, this baroque guffaw will clean the chemo-

therapy and radiation from your own mental pollution.

Clock Radio:
> Twelve noon in Havana, Cuba
> nine in the morning in San Francisco, USA
> eight at night in Moscow
> eleven at night in Hanoi, Vietnam
> midnight in Peking
> midnight in Ulan Bator, Mongolia
> eleven in the morning in Mexico City
> seven at night in Paris

Gold, the stones of Tulum; gold, the fine stone...; gold, the house, the study, the lights; gold this sky, golden echo, gold (our) suitcases, our thirst. Knee upon the earth. Gold, work; gold, the clock.... This, this Time.

Green nature, delicious green-blue waters of the tropics; far off, behind, the disaster, that *agony of persecutions and irritations boldly imposed*.... With you, the Meeting. From the shadows to the Light. From the sinuous spider web of the imagination to the kiss

> sharp tongue (all the befores, except today, Lisandro
> our Silver Anniversary...in a crystal
> pyramid) this tongue
> no longer disappears
> it is a bird
> it flies
> and retreats
> and can reaffirm
> the intensity
> of its flight

> moistened tongue
> spread

with fear, with
pine nuts

tarragon tongue, dancing
suspended in the sky
of your mouth

*...a before and an after, a closing and parting of curtains. An empty theatre.
[...] How hot it is!*

I imagine those figures as Andalusian screams, retouched, beautiful, yes, wearing imaginary women's clothing, made flesh today in the ghetto The California, Hammel Alley, at a corner in the center of the city or in Old Havana...I hear the body's music, from the gut.... But, ah, I project my hip like this, twist my waist (me?), toss a shoulder like this...project my other hip in continuous movement in the opposite direction, palpitate (me?); one arm like the handle of a jar, palm facing back, the other hand in the air like someone leaving. And here I move my neck, open my mouth and my head, a mythic poetic world perfectly balanced on dark vertebra.... What? *What* emerges from my mouth. It will emerge without prior command, independent of my will. It is true, my *true nature explodes with overwhelming force.*

No pork! No eggplant, no potatoes, no peppers, no tomatoes... (none of the more than 500 nightshades), no spinach, no beats, no dairy, no sugar, no chocolate... No dyes or preservatives, caffeine never. That's right: *fanatical, fundamentalist.* Like you never were, could not be, in times of plenty.

So then? Authentic quinoa. Cold ground Chia seeds (strengthen the muscles, repair the tissue...; high performance for your mind, your heart: your two governing bodies most worthy of being One). Sesame, a natural tonic, symbol of fertility in the East and certainly food for longevity. But is the nutritional process so simple, so general, that purely personal factors shouldn't be considered? "Please, eat carrots, not carotene," master Suu comically recommends. The secret is

simple: it is contained in Silence. Silence, serenity, concentration. The act of loving oneself. The temple that is your body demands it. You give it the marvelous capsule that is a fruit, a seed. Open, Sesame!

Cheek to Cheek

I see my dress floating on the red tide, tossed by a wind like five propellers. I must take my clothes from the closet, I want to emerge from my corset. Hanging it up, I smooth it: feel its surface as if engaged in a medical examination, leading with my nose. I touch its embroidery, its smooth seams, its zipper's long pilgrimage. The pads of my fingers lose themselves in that row of quiet teeth, that yesterday opened to receive our body, imprisoning it like a round mollusk, like a medallion or locket.

I slide the zipper that climbs without tripping. We enter the suit again. The old *partenaire* has asked us to dance again, without worrying about the size of our slippers. Nervously I zip and unzip. Laughter comes...and that feeling in the gut. Is this a sled or a morning for skiing in Moscow? Is it the climb to Tulum: proud on the reef, facing the sea? Is it the emotion of Palms? The vertigo of the Eiffel Tower, the Degas in the Orsay, the lights of the Champs Elysees?

A spider web of little lights hangs with its rattlesnake sound over the Grand Theater. The sound of voices blends with the pulsing timbre of my raucous laughter. Anchorless, weightless, light, we part cleavage/the zipper: free of the leotard, the tutu and the slippers' ribbons, the braids of memory severed.

Along Brazo, splendid, Carruana... *Cheek to cheek*. High heels. Wood against the foot. Let your body go, let down your hair, loosen your tongue. One turn and another and another on your own body rising.... Me?

The table stretches like a banquet. I don't want to make myself dizzy, I don't want to fall, I don't look down. The dark green water makes it impossible to see what I imagine. Look straight ahead, I tell myself. Do not slip on the moss. Do not fall in the dream. The cracked floorboards. They shatter and come apart. The unsteady rhythm

barely sustains me. Earrings and souvenirs of hasty letters, the last book you borrowed, float between the boards. This is waste water. You must lose weight if you want to cross over, empty the sand of sacks, put cucumber slices in your ears so you can see better.

In a single motion you pull out the drawers and advance on happy toes. You delight in the crash of the last porcelains, the bright colors of the pencils, the infinite variations of your Murano paperweight. Awkward, you lift your leg to spin again. *Mejilla con mejilla.* Cheek to cheek. The cyclone takes all the rest to the water: all the weights that steadied your head, sustained your foundation. Free of counterweights, one leg to one side, the other to the other. Your work table finally clean.

Upon the naked board, two clocks. That persistent perfume returns.

Those who so furiously applaud the gift of equilibrium, the crossing over, do not know what this return means. The mirror has turned. You announce *Pomp and Circumstance.* You announce the *Song of the Israelites.* You look with pride at the orderly world of your table and sit at last.

An orchid. A bouquet of mauve tulips.

To Heian Perón Araújo and Loipa Araújo Carruana

Lía Villares

Hunger for Clarity

Strip of light.
ghost-ridden crossroads, leafmold paradise.
—Adrienne Rich[9]

something. Expropriating the world and winking at you from the other side of an inevitable ocean: another old room in Central Havana: a bit of window and unique sea—always the same—or vice-versa. Nothing. She, nothing. She stays—it's me myself, we are—floating for a while and waking in the foam at the edge. Most of the time the waves didn't allow for sleep; and when she slept she dreamt of the city beneath the sea, swallowed to her last tired breath. On the other side of the street, the man shouting bread, avocado and sunflowers shakes me and got *us* up quickly. The obligatory yawn. We. We had to brush off our soul and toss it like a dream out the window to that street in movement at unthinkable hours, goings-without-comings: dilapidated time and the noise of motors invading the esophagus. All of it too inappropriate. All of it too, all?

Adrienne: *I know you are reading this poem/ standing up in a bookstore far from the ocean/ [...] and the open valise speaks of flight/ but you cannot leave yet [...] I know you are reading this poem in a waiting room/ of eyes met and unmeeting, of identity with strangers./ [...] in the boredom and fatigue of the young who are counted out/ count themselves out at too young an age.*[10]

9. "What Kind of Times are These" from *Collected Poems: 1950-2012. Dark Fields of the Republic: Poems 1991-1995* (W. W. Norton and Company Inc., 1995)

10. Lines from *An Atlas of the Difficult World.*

dust. There is so much dust. I breathe it constantly. I remove it and do nothing but clean it a little again only for it to fall once more upon the piano and books, covering them again and again and reaching my lungs and then I breathe it out again and it's always like that. Mother complains about the dust. *Tus peines sur mon Coeur et vos pieds sur une chaise*, She sings. A stain emerges from the painting. It almost reaches the wall, I suddenly lose sight of it. I have no one to look at or anything, in any case, but. Eyes. A face in triplicate. Six gazes multiplied in the mirrors. I am dying of sleeplessness, insomnia, even asleep I die of exhaustion. We die. Marks upon my body. Each time I bathe and pay attention I discover new marks: scratches near my buttocks, scabs that She picks again and again there is always a lot of blood, bruises left by unquestionable blows I didn't notice. We interrupt Mother's bath; she forgot to lock the door. She hesitates, feels indifference—in the mirror—and finally grief. We become sorrowful. Mosquitos. Each day light floods this room and they are still there, thirsty, getting flattened beneath my noisy palm, use-less. Trains. They follow one another through our early morning hours of insomnia, become part of the night, complete nothingness, like the slow clock and the end of the *jazz corner*—insipid date for a radio audience that doesn't sleep—. Like my progressive blindness reading Kerouac in such bad light, like Mother's yellow lamp in the next room, like the pure murmur of her voice. She spells out loud almost everything she thinks. We hear the separate letters that seem like disconnected, unfinished, phrases. Articulate the words to disarticulate their meanings, the essence implicit or not in each. The insipidness of all the moments without. Mother nods off. She yawns. We the sleeping ones.

Adrienne: *Imagine a city where nothing/ is forgiven [...] the precise reason for the shaving of the confused girl's head [...] a city memory starved but intent on retributions/ [...] tell me if it is not true you still live in that city./ [...] I have forced myself to come back like a daughter/ required to put her mother's house in order.*[11]

11. Lines from "Rusted Legacy," 1997.

interpretation. I began reading old mail I collect like random samples, fragments of frozen time. Time is butter, we said in unison with a grimace that seemed like laughter. A chiclet, a placebo state. People left out, people blurred and unknown; everyone in the world is someone different and they don't show until they are conscious of themselves. Who were they? Who...am I? Do I have a country? An island? Isolated. I am like Her; we come from the same place and spin in the same direction. Disarticulated Mother. By shattering the clocks with a hammer, you say, you can kill time; and if we then spread a little butter on top.... Slowly go through the mirror. And then trap a certain calm in a little cup of steaming coffee Mother brings us.

Adrienne. *This me—should she, should she lay beneath an oxidized scab/ stuffed with memory in a place/ of small anecdotes no one left/ to gather the whole history [hysteria] of dissidence? [...] —only for yourself? each of us has a city embedded.*

inanity, Her. Hurry, us. Delay, Mother. A long wail, farther away, a desperate feline call, a sign of something, surely, something immediate, unnamable, unforeseen. The hollow space of an object-thing (house) that has dis-appeared, pulls at my sight. I am thinking of an answer that never engenders a question, an enormous bubble emerges from your hair, it doesn't manage to expel the soapy water. We are in the bathtub. My juggling subconscious plays with the memory of a decomposing fruit, a warm rain and many feet all together, each of them different. I reflect a little on this profound, almost autistic, egotism, we emit as if from a shower. To be inside oblivion itself when this happens, an unstoppable murmur of voices, an uncomfortable embrace, *the stockings make me hot....* To write from within the dream, return from time to time, listen. It's all there where we don't see it. What did I have to think about now, what was I thinking about, *had* to think about. Mother complains. I despair. She vomits a deaf scream in pantomime. Before. Never. Before closing her eyes. Once again. We are cold and I do not know how to cover us, I have scattered ideas, they lose themselves like the chord of an oxidized harmonica.

Only the dog barking at a ghost in the dark is still there, the girl—Mother—folding sheets in a patio full of creeping orchids. A rapid cough. An enormous penis. More mosquitoes. We are in a crowd at a funeral home. The sofa springs sound each time someone gets up so someone else can take their place. There aren't enough benches for so many people. In the ruins of the crumpled building, cats. She speaks to me: *this is, almost, the imprecise sound.* I feel her clear voice although her lips remain still. The wait, Mother. The anxiety, ourselves. The calm. Her. Finalities.

Adrienne. *[Human thing]. For a human animal to call for help/ on another animal/ [...] into the birth-yell of the yet-to-be-human child/ pushed out of the woman the yet-to-be woman.*[12]

one day so much *tempo* in delicious outpouring and the other, unattainable now. Perpetual present. The need for acceptance. Mother. Uncertainty. Her. Conformity, us. Counting obsessions. Certainty of memory? Vagueness as artifact. Errors, us. Neurosis, Mother. Her, laziness... I read and delight in my narcissistic dissatisfaction, in my loss, in my lost music. I must take care not to tangle the crystals in the rattle's threads—made of tiny painted pieces, from the globe lamp that was pushed to the floor—. Eyelids opening and closing intermittently. Coltrane spits incoherent phrases now, cuts them, frag-ments them. Attentively we listen to the piano's entrance and saxophone's applause. Paralysis. Importance. Drawing in slow motion the non-history, non-action, non-narrative. I walk in zig-zag and then in a straight line. She goes in circles. We all dream this common language. To walk toward, to, the house. My house. Ours. Once again the radio ("ah, at last, don't forget it, please, don't ever forget it: defend your smile!") Mother announcer. In a bad time a worse face, they keep reminding us again and again. Despair and more dust. *Quelqu'n.* Ink, Miles Davis. Corricone, Patience, us. Dawn, Her. Sterility, us. Strangeness, Mother. Calluses on my feet. Need to urinate, to hear someone whistling at me, need of the same in different gazes, differ-

12. Lines from "Fox," *Fox: Poemas* 1998-2000.

ent desires. Chipped walls, always static. Thirst. Us. Verticality, but no: better to maintain horizontality. Relief, Her. Noise, Mother. Darkness, Us. Drops falling and wood that creaks in Mother's nearby door, her uninterrupted signs; her dress hanging in the middle of the room, dancing with the curtain on the balcony clothesline. Circular movement of the experience. Her. Machines of desire. Us. Repetition, *ad infinitum.* The sameness of being.

Adrienne. *To live, to lie awake/ at an hour when nothing can be done/ to further any decision/ [...] imagining the existence/ of something uncreated/ this poem/ our lives.*[13]

13. Lines from "Incipience," 1973.

Zurelys López Amaya

Anna's Secret

To Nikita S. Mijalkov

We'll see what happens. Nothing is the same as what is discovered one day and undone the next. Light floods us and we are extinguished in obscurity. What discovers us is the passion of day and night moving through childhood's magic doors and the innocence of pleasure.

From the depth of my thoughts something interrupts me. The memories are almost always withered, compensating decisions yet to be taken, betraying secrets kept for years and which then emerge desperate to tell their stories lost in time.

I am Anna. The little girl filmed by her father, Nikia Sergéievich Mijalkov, from her sixth to eighteenth year, and to whom each year he repeated the same question:

—What are you afraid of?

—I am afraid of the dark, of my teachers, of the rides at the amusement park, of the dentist, the boogey man who carries children off forever, of bridges, of caves and their humidity, of snakes, of noises in the night, of voices I hear but do not see, of heights, of clowns with their bulging eyes who stare at me as if they are having fun.

Everything seems strange. I am Anna. I had a happy infancy. My childhood was about jumping over things, especially walls. One day I decided to jump the wall in the courtyard of my house, the next day the neighbor's wall. On the way to school I skipped over the paving stones so I wouldn't have to step on the lines. I heard voices:

—*Step on a line, eat a frog.*

Can you imagine eating frogs all the time? Disgusting! I hate frogs that are different and not in their places. I think everything should have an order to it, although in the end nothing is perfect.

My elementary school is called Domingo Lence. I never knew why. I guess it's the name of a revolutionary martyr. The only thing I knew, because I was curious, is that it was built over a cemetery, and that they found some strange earth insects there that seemed like some sort of worm with a hard shell that we grabbed from below and when we asked which was South or North, they would point in the right direction. It was a strange thing, but when you are a child adults rarely believe what you say.

Everything was fine until one day when we were playing with those insects during school recess. Francis, the little boy who had a glass eye because of an accident he'd suffered at home, asked one of the insects Rosa had in her hand:

—Where is Anna?

The insect with no eyes turned toward me and pointed as if accusing me of something. Francis asked it again, and when the insect finished going around the circle it stood straight up, looking eyeless at the sky. Then he came back to me, pointing with its accusing finger as if it was the school's principal. That was the last time I played in the patio. I kept on jumping my walls without stepping on the infinite lines on my way home. Even today it's hard for me to step on them.

Each year Nikita asked the same question:

—What are you afraid of?

I am afraid of the dark, of bridges, of heights, of caves and their humidity, of airplanes, of clowns, of noises when I sleep, and of death.

—Why are you afraid of clowns?

Because I've discovered they are sad, I've seen them cry to entertain others, but really they are very sad.

Nothing happens without a reason. We are, and at the same time we are nothing compared with nature which is the true being.

The truth is, I am not Anna, but since I always wanted to be, now I am.

The blackouts were more unbearable all the time. There was an uncle who each year took me in his car to meet part of the family. When I was twenty I learned that uncle was my father. A rebel who

came down from the Sierra Maestra and we couldn't talk about him because everything was a big secret.

I didn't have television until I was nine. I watched the cartoons at a neighbor's house, but one day I mashed the four fingers of my left hand when I slammed her door so she wouldn't bother me again. Horrors! A little girl screams in her trembling for the four broken fingers without nails. I saw stars and everything with the cartoon characters.

Then I lost consciousness, and when I came too I had a television set. I think God was there, or maybe my uncle.

My father and my green uncle were one and the same. When he showed up he would say things like: "How big you are! How are you doing at school? Do you want to take a ride in the car? What do you want to be when you grow up?" And I would answer:

—Nothing.

—Well, nothing is something—he would say.

If Nikita asked me: "What are you afraid of?" I would answer:

—Of a little girl called Yurién, who hits me at school and throws stones. Like a desperate child, I once thought if she died it would be the best thing that could happen. Even her family would know peace. And then one day she did die. I had to go to a psychologist with my mother because almost every day I dreamed I had killed her.

When I was a child I did the opposite of what everyone wanted. Played with the boys, told a lot of lies, climbed trees, made up stories so I could survive in the neighborhood where everyone except me knew who my father was. I always knew there was a secret I had to discover.

Sometimes, on my way to school, I talked to a grandfather who gave me money to buy ice cream boats. The grandfather didn't speak, he just gave me the money I later exchanged for delicious chocolate ice cream. The best ice cream in the world. Even though I asked him a lot of questions, he always answered with signs. I decided he must be mute.

One fine day, seated on our bench, I waited a long time for him, but he didn't show up. I went looking for him. I asked for him at the

house where they told me he lived. A very old woman answered the door and called someone else to talk to me because she was an invalid. When I asked about the old man, describing him because he'd never told me his name, the old woman began to cry so hard I got scared. And the other, who was younger, asked me in desperation: But where have you seen him? I explained that he gave me money for ice cream, and that every day he waited for me when I got out of school. I stood in the doorway and pointed at the bench where we sat.

They both tried to ask me more questions, but couldn't because they were crying too hard. Then the younger woman told me that he had died four years before. I didn't understand anything. And even though I felt bad for them, I ran off like the light I was talking about at the beginning, or like a soul carried by the devil. For a long time this confused me, and I tried to forget by avoiding buying ice cream with someone else's money.

Jumping isn't the only way one can survive. As the years passed, Nikita continued to ask me the same question:

—What are you afraid of?

And I responded:

—I am afraid of death, of heights, of darkness, of lies, of reality, of change and of secrets.

—Why?

—Because I've discovered that fantasy doesn't exist. I don't like reality. I don't like death because it is the end of everything good and bad, and we still don't know if another life exists. I'm also afraid of change. It's almost always bad. And I don't like secrets.

—Why?

—Because you discover secrets you didn't want to know, because I don't like it when things change. I like them the way they are. If they change I will feel very sad, and I don't like being sad.

One day, when I turned nine, the mother of my first father, meaning my siblings' father, the one I was supposed to call "Grandmother Dominga," took me to the mirror in her room, took my head in her hands and pushed it hard against the glass, telling me with anguish:

—Look at yourself! Do you even think you look like my son? You are not his daughter. You are the daughter of a communist who came down from the Sierra.

When I got home I looked in the mirror again and began to search for a resemblance with all the men who passed by my street. Nothing could ever be the same.

To be Anna, and answer all Nikita's questions, makes me see things differently. It's like having one body and being in another, at the same time, as life demands that you respond to things as you can.

Olga Marta Pérez

I Am the One with the Ribbons

María Little Ribbons went to take a bath,
she left her ribbons in the banana grove...
—Folk Song

Sometimes, from my observation perch in the mango tree, I look at the small village where I was born and where I have played up to now. Nothing has ever happened here, nothing has come; not wars, not the railroad. This has its advantages, like my grandmother says, because bad news doesn't come either. And I think also good news, but I don't know much about that since I haven't heard any, I don't know what good or bad news would be.

A butterfly would be something else, I better get down, I've eaten enough mangoes and am going to bathe in the river. It occurred to a very serious man, among the first who built their houses by the river, to put up a sign I don't know how to read. But since I have a good memory my grandmother told me it said there that this village was built piece by piece out of necessity, without order but with very good will. The truth is the serious man had a lot of words in his head, but there were so many that he couldn't be easily understood. Good will, who knows what good will is.

I think, and my grandmother and the neighbors agree, that the great event in this village, the greatest, was my birth on November 9, 1888 at six in the morning. I was the first child born in this village of necessity. I saw the light in this place and the event might have taken place with neither shame nor glory, except that after me some hundred little ones came along...just like that, as if the wonder of life decided to take place in every corner of the village, on the river bank or in the grove where the perfume of fruit makes you dizzy.

My grandmother Teodora tells me my mother died in childbirth. That's why, when I go by, the neighbors whisper: "she is an orphan, poor thing," but when grandmother goes by they don't say anything. Could it be that they have no name for her although she has no child? How strange, no name for her...

Ah! There's the river. That's also important. We wash in the river, get water for the house, baptize the children like they did with me who, nine days old and without a hair on my head, they named Baldomera María. Grandma says I just cried and cried. Of course, with that ugly name they gave me.... Now I'm going to bathe to calm myself, like when I was little, my grandma put me in the water to cure my tantrums. The truth is, I get over my tears and sadness among these sweet-smelling guava trees, eating apple bananas off the stalk and looking for what I've never found: butterfly nests.

Teodora is calling me. She must be standing at the backdoor of the house with her flip-flop in her hand, threatening the air or empty words, it doesn't matter. But I'm not going back until I forget the awful laughter and taunts at school: "Baldy, baldy, baldy." That's why I hit them. The worst thing is that the teacher didn't even ball them out, but she too will find out who Baldomera María is when her desk is covered with stink flowers.

It's true that for a long time I didn't have a hair on my head and I suffered a lot because of that, because people think children don't suffer those things. Well, I say they do, we suffer when people make fun of us—grandma and her hard words—, like when my little bird died or when Alicia stopped making us molasses candy at noon because her hands got stiff.

But I have hair now! My grandma couldn't stand it anymore and last night she called the drummers, and before the morning mist she picked herbs in the mountains that she took to the edge of the waters, along with stones and shells and saints, and at dawn made a great ceremony at the river. One drum could be heard as soon as the sun came up and the spirits woke and danced. We'd never seen anything like it, they were so funny. I can still see them coming around the bluish stone where Teodora stood me. Then the biggest came, grandma

spoke strange words to the sky, to the clouds, to the roots of the trees, and the water she sprinkled on my head was cold and scented. I don't think I'll ever forget that mixture of scents. Good thing the sun came out right away and warmed me, but the most important thing: I got hair! And I once again understood my grandmother's words when she said: "You've got hair now."

Ha! What hair, rebellious little wires, and she had to use lots of coco butter and a comb to make these small pigtails that changed my name. I'm not mad, but happy, because I'm not bald anymore, and my little ponytails with their red ribbons are cute. Teodora says I am beautiful, she must feel very sorry for me or love me more than usual. And tomorrow I'm going to school in a better mood, and afterwards the kids and I are going to collect mangoes on Chivo Hill or at Indian Cave. I won't pay attention to them even if they sing the new ditty they've invented. Is it because they love me, or because they are happy, or because they feel sorry for me? It's all the same to me, I have pigtails now and even if the neighbors whisper—it must be so I won't suffer—that I'm an orphan, I have a magical grandmother and that's a lot.

Now I eat some bananas before I bathe, there's a mature stalk hidden away, so well hidden not even the mockingbirds have discovered it, I'm going to mark it with one of my red ribbons. Grandmother Teodora told me bananas are noble fruits and you shouldn't take a knife to them but break apart their skin with your fingers, that it's best to let them ripen on the stalk so the tree can feed them to the very last minute. Although they sometimes get ants, I know that very well because ants are great explorers, they discover everything and eat everything too, the truth is, ants aren't sorry for anything.

Thinking long and hard about everything that's happened to me in these eight years of mine, I still believe I am the most important thing that's happened in this village built from necessity, not only because of all the other births but because of that ditty even the parrots repeat from the moment they wake up: *Pigtail María went to take a bath....* Okay, I'm going to bathe and I'll leave my ribbons in the banana grove to scare the mockingbirds that have no compassion.

Mylene Fernández Pintado

Sprüngli

For Lil, Carole and Amay

—I wish *I* could manage to be glad—the Queen said—only I never can remember the rule. You must be very happy living in this wood and being glad whenever you like!

—Only it is so *very* lonely here!—Alice said in a melancholy voice; and at the thought of her loneliness two large tears came rolling down her cheeks.

—*Through the Looking Glass*, Lewis Carroll

—Tickets, please—said the Conductor, sticking his head through the little window. In a moment, everyone handed over their tickets.

—Come on, young lady, show me your ticket—repeated the Conductor, looking at me angrily. And a great number of voices in unison said:—Don't keep us waiting, young lady, his time is worth a thousand francs a minute.

—My name is Alice—I introduced myself, and added somewhat frightened—, I'm afraid I didn't buy the ticket to Sprüngli. There was no ticket window where I come from.

—Her name is Alice and there's no ticket window where she comes from—the passengers said again, all together.

—Don't give me excuses, young lady—said the Conductor. And the chorus added: —Don't say anything at all, young lady. Language costs a thousand francs a word.

The Conductor took a newspaper and began dividing it among the passengers.

—If you want a copy for yourself, you'll have to travel first class—the Conductor said in an almost friendly tone—. Here, in coach, there's only one newspaper for all the passengers. The first row reads the front page and so forth, those interested in sports or culture sit in the back, those worried about the market in the middle and those interested in politics up front. But—he said as if catching himself in a fault—I've already spoken with you for more than a minute.

—Thank you, that's what I wanted to know—I said, nervously.

—Good, although you're not from around here, I can see you're a decent young lady so I'll give you one last bit of free information. If you pay extra in first class you can read the next day's news.

—The future!?

—Yes, the truth is it's not as unpredictable as you think—here the Conductor made a gesture of weariness and at that moment he seemed to me to be only a tired little old man, proud of discharging his duty.

I got comfortable in my window seat and the train pulled out. Before my eyes, like photo stills, paraded gothic villages, churches, mountains, waterfalls, lakes, fields and woods. It's like a movie, a post-card or the colored top of a box of chocolates—I thought—. Is this what Sprüngli will be like?

I didn't know anyone what had been to Sprüngli, although every-one boasted about having eaten the famous chocolates. They said they were made with cocoa and imported workers and chocolate masters using local recipes jealously guarded in the vault at a secret bank. Sprüngli was the city of chocolate.

The train stopped at a station that was nothing more than a tick-et office and a big clock. The Conductor ordered all the passengers to leave the cars for thirty-one minutes. To avoid my travel companions and their chorus of sermons, I decided to walk to a field that looked as if it were dotted with multicolor spots. As I drew near, I discovered a small army of people carrying small and large brushes and jars of paint in different colors.

The first group painted the grass.—It's the most difficult—their leader told me, wanting me to think his brigade's work the most

important—. The grass must be even but look natural, the paint mustn't splash the blade beside it, because then this one would be greener than the other. And if it rains tomorrow, we will have to come back and paint it darker, and if it doesn't rain for a few days, we'll have to look for ochre tones so we can paint dry grass. As you can see, it's not an easy task. I have always been very careful and demanding in this work. Next week they'll promote me to buyer. It's the best position; instead of being here painting each blade of grass, I'll go to the city to choose the colors.

—That group you see over there—he continued telling me in a confidential way—paints the flowers, they fancy themselves artists, even call themselves impressionists. They are all from the Mediterranean, badly organized and believe in inspiration instead of discipline.

The "impressionists" seemed more amusing. One of them was painting some blue roses while the others, seated on the grass, gave him advice and discussed the hue.

—In the end it's all the same, we'll have to forget about such ideas and paint the flowers according to our instructions. No one here wants to lose his job—one of them said.

—Or be sent to paint the cows—said the one next to him.

—The cows? How does one paint a cow?

—Oh, you're a very ignorant young lady, I can tell you're not from around here—answered the one who was painting the blue flowers, without ceasing to admire his work—. It's very simple, you must live with the cows, day and night, until you're accustomed to their presence, each day you get closer until one of them lets you caress her. Once that happens, you're able to walk alongside at her pace and paint the black or brown spots, as you're told. But it's very boring. The cows only speak Dutch and they're very stingy, they never offer you a glass of milk. That work is always done by those who come from the uninteresting areas, like you. Except that you're very short to be able to walk among cows.

—Do you do this all year long?—I managed to ask in the midst of my astonishment.

—Of course, except that in winter we only use white to give the surface a covering of snow. Those who work with the cows don't have work then because they take them to covered corrals. Since nobody sees them there, it doesn't matter what color they are.

I would like to have known if they also painted the dusks and dawns, the sky and rain clouds, and if, in the end, it turned out that the waterfalls were simply made of water that someone spilled from the mountaintops, but I was afraid the train would leave without me. I said goodbye to the group that continued pondering the blue flowers, and ran to the station.

The train traveled effortlessly, the passengers read their pages and the loudspeakers indicated the stops coming up and those we'd left behind. Also the hour and date, the season of the year and temperature, the tide and phase of the moon, how the stock market was doing and the monetary exchange rate for the day.

Arriving at Sprüngli, I noticed that all the signs began with the words IT IS PROHIBITED. The list of prohibitions was infinite. It included everything from IT IS PROHIBITED TO EAT OR DRINK IN THE STREET to IT IS PROHIBITED TO STEP ON FROGS OR SEA URCHINS.

After attentively reading the signs, I was relieved. Eating chocolates wasn't against the law, but there was no sign advertising a store where they could be purchased. The streets were flanked by majestic gray buildings, the names of which didn't indicate anything tantalizing or fun. I finally decided to enter one that had, at the entrance, the head of a cat with a big joyous smile.

—Good day. Is this a chocolate store?—I asked a thin man who wasn't smiling like the sign on the door.

—Good day, are you insured?—the man asked me.

—No, I'm not sure, that's why I'm asking—I said.

—I'm not asking if you're sure but if you're insured. This is an insurance company. The biggest in the world, and so our work is the most important in the world. For example, I could sue you for asking stupid questions and making me lose time, focus on my work, money and even my job. If I became unemployed for

attending to your stupid questions instead of my very important work, I could also ask for indemnification and you would be forced to pay me as well: rent, bills, insurance and taxes. But if you were insured against damages and prejudices caused by third parties if they ask stupid questions, your insurance company would take care of it all.

—I don't know what an insurance is, but it seems very important—I hesitated.

—Of course it's important. Do you know that memory works in two directions?—asked the man with a satisfied air.

—I see they also make jokes here—I thought with relief, and I placed my elbow on the counter, more confidently—. No, I had no idea. I think mine only works backwards.

—That's because you're not from around here, and your memory is so bad it only goes in one direction. Ours moves forward and back, and that's the principle of insurance. To remember what is going to happen.

—To insure you means covering all the risks of your future life, to be freed from all your errors, to be forgiven in advance for the sins you might commit—the man began his speech, very inspired—. For example: I can issue you a policy for damage to extinct species in the polar regions, and every month you pay me a certain amount in case one day you wound an Emperor Penguin in the Antarctic.

—I don't think I'm ever going to the Antarctic and even less would I harm an Emperor Penguin. Why should I pay for something I'll never do?—I asked myself over and over after saying goodbye to the man who was still very serious.

The chocolate store was next door, and no one smiled on the sign at the entrance.

—What do you want to buy?—asked the saleswoman.

—I'm not sure yet—I said in a friendly tone—. First I'd like to take a look around, if I may.

—If you want you can look straight ahead and to both sides—the saleswoman said—, but not all around unless you have eyes at the back of your neck.

As I did not have them, I contented myself with making the rounds and looking at the shelves as I approached them. The store seemed to be filled with chocolates of all sorts, sizes and shapes, but each time I stopped before a showcase and tried to pick one of the bonbons up and examine its contents in detail, it was completely empty, while all the others were overflowing.

—It's a new sales method, this way you will always come back looking for more chocolates, because the one you really want will disappear before your eyes, explained the saleswoman.

—It's very tiring to live in Sprüngli—I sighed resignedly and contented myself with looking at the ones that were behind the counter without trying to touch them.

—It's not tiring, it's expensive—the saleswoman explained.

I bought a small box of chocolates that seemed the least expensive. I left, walking among drab buildings and worried people wearing gloves and carrying briefcases and cellphones.

I looked for a trash can where I could dispose of the cellophane that encased the box. I found a group of metal cans, hermetically sealed by hatches also made of metal, on which a series of digital letters read: Alternate garbage pickup. Exclusive licenses for neighbors of numbers 1,234 to 2,341.

—How do they know that only the neighbors from those numbers throw their garbage here?—I asked myself, without taking my eyes from the cans.

The reply came immediately. A woman, carrying bags of different colors, placed her hand at an angle on the surface of each of the cans and waited until something showed up on the screen. Then she introduced a card and read more information. As soon as she did, she deposited each bag of garbage in a different bin.

—Excuse me. Where can I find a can to throw away this wrapper?—I asked, after watching the entire routine in astonishment.

—Are you a citizen? Resident? Scholarship student? Black market worker? Do you have a border contract?—the woman asked.

My name is Alice, and I don't think I am any of those, I just came to Sprüngli to buy chocolates.

—Then you are a tourist. You must go to see the cashier at one of the banks and pay the surcharge that gives you the right to dirty our city with the wrappers of what you eat. Then, look for the appropriate bins, they say tourist on them, but you can only use the one that has a number on its digital list identical to the number on the card they gave you at the bank. After that, you will have to check the cubic centimeters you've used against what the card permits. That's how you will know how much garbage you can throw out during your stay in Sprüngli. The second card will cost double, the third triple, and so forth. You will see that it's the best method so that tourists don't poison Sprüngli with their chocolate papers.

—Thank you—I said, feeling alluded to. I'll look for a bank to buy that card.

—If you need help, don't hesitate to call me, I'm on the tourist information line. You can sign up if you go to the bank and buy a credit card for calls....

I kept nodding before the avalanche of instructions, even though I was no longer listening. When the woman turned her back and began walking way, I walked in the opposite direction to make sure I didn't run into her again. —This city doesn't seem very big—I thought, as I sat on a bench fingering the bag of chocolates.

I opened the box and began to eat each praline, stuffing the wrappings in my pockets. When I'd finished the last one, after having tasted flavors I didn't know existed, my coat pockets were full of little papers: silver, gold, red, blue, orange, green, violet, brown, pink and gray, all with a giant S in the center.

I looked around, searching for a trashcan for tourists, but didn't find one.

Well, it's not the end of the world. I'll throw them away when I get home. And the word *home* almost melted in my mouth, sweet and warm, like the best of Sprüngli's chocolates.

Montagnola, April 2009

Rocío Santillana

Havana Club

Fired for sabotaging the interests of tourism and the country's economy.

—Holy God, Isabel, that's an embarrassment to our lineage and it might even create diplomatic conflicts.

—Don't be stupid, Dude. Everyone knows I don't drink.

—Okay, Daughter, but a contract is a contract.

—Come on, think about it, I never signed anything saying I had to pose downing a bottle of rum. Never. And thanks to the fact that I was willing to be in the photo with my skirt just above the knee. I am not my sister; she's the one with all the nerve.

—Leave your sister out of this, she's never done anything to you.

—She hasn't? Look, we are twins, but one of us is very, I mean very, different from the other. I'd just gone out the door, my eyes shooting sparks from the rage I felt, when she came in. Did she console me? Noooooooo. She almost knocked me over as she went by. Because she came in losing it, full of herself, and everyone falling at her feet, adoring her as if she was The One.

—You've always been a little jealous.

—She opened the long jacket she was wearing, and paid no attention to the Calatrava Cross, or the insignia, or your lineage or ancestry or anything. She just took everything off and got naked then and there. What do you think of that?

—I think your sister is her own person, but she's not capable of that.

—Well, not completely naked, but stripped down to her bikini.

—I told you. See? It's not the same.

She grabbed a glass of rum and, glub, she drank the whole thing down in one swallow, and then she said: Here's to the new image of Havana Club. Right in front of me, with no shame!

—Wait. Did you say bikini? And you didn't do anything to stop her?

—Of course! But then she said: *Don't you tell me nothing, what happens, happens....* And it happened. Needless to say, it happened.

—What happened?

—They hired her right under my nose. Listen, my sister is anything but easy.

—Okay, but you'd quit.

—Quit, no. They fired me, and so they could hire my own sister. Damned woman!

Don't blame her. It's bad enough the poor thing's locked up in that dungeon surrounded by rotting and oxidized old cannons. For once she got out.

—*Ay, how little you know about life, Papa, how mistaken you are.* In the first place, my sister loves living among cannons.

—Don't begin with that, I know what you're going to say.

—In the second place, every night she frequents much worse dungeons. But everywhere: where the P 5 dies, where they train the boxers...

—I've said, it's worth it.

—Where you catch the 400 and ride like sardines to the Eastern Beaches along with all those suburbanites from Old Havana. Back and forth, that's where your dear daughter goes every night and then home to her dungeon delighted with cannons that are even blacker and aren't the least bit oxidized. The only thing oxidized are those bed springs of hers I hear every single night.... I mean every single night. Listen, that girl doesn't stop, even when she's on the rag. Fuck, no one gets any sleep.

—Okay, Isabel, enough already. Each of us is how we are.

—And you defend her, because the girl gets it from you. You think I don't know, all those trips from Havana to Las Palmas in the Canary Islands? It's not clothing for resale you come back with, and you talk about lineage. Not even a gift for your daughter. I've been wearing this renaissance dress since I'm fifteen.

—Shut up, don't go off on one of your tangents, we're talking about your sister. Her place is right here, in the watchtower, looking

out at the bay, graceful and clever as she's always been.

—Okay, wait one minute. What you telling me? That she's bad at what she does? That the Castle of the Royal Straightjacket is too big for me? Are you calling me a scarecrow? Or I'm less of your daughter than that shameless hussy? That prig who does nothing and earns the same as me, including royalties and picture rights? And after today, just imagine.

—No, Isabel, you do a stupendous job, but your sister is the oldest.

—Enough with the abuses, fucker, we're twins.

—But your mother had her a few minutes before she had you.

—Enough of your lies, it's a miracle you even know who the mother of your daughters is, you must have fucked 'em all: *You never gave a damn, sticking it any old place.*

—A little respect, Isabel, I'm your father.

—Which is exactly why I know you, and no one sees my sister during the day, I mean, in the trade. No one sees her up here in the tower, working her ass off hauling metal.

—Well, she's never been able to deal with her allergy to the sun.

—Oh my god, how long do we have to listen all that allergy crap? Stop it already, she got over that a long time ago, don't forget we live in the country that's at the international vanguard of medical treatments.

—Don't exaggerate, she just got out of the hospital. Isabel is convalescing.

—When it's in her interest. It's me you see slaving away, day and night, cyclones or no cyclones, for gringos and for domestic tourism alike, in this historic patrimony of humanity.

—That voluntary cooperative is what's fucked us over. Because you get paid in CUCs, and I wouldn't be surprised if one of these days you get paid in Euros, you've got the Historian in your pocket and I know how you take advantage of him. What do you think: this is the Perricholi's romance with the Peruvian Viceroy? This isn't Peru. This is Cuba, and everyone wants to leave this place. Even the foreigners when they catch on, me included, and I've done my bit for History. So pack your bags, I'm taking you back to Spain if I have to slap you silly first.

—What are you saying? I don't see any gringos around here. At best, one of your ancestors was from the Canaries and communed with screwballs, but you were born right here under a Ceiba. Come on, let me see your carnet.

—What carnet, what shit!

—Citizen, your carnet.

—Stop sticking your finger in my face and talking like that, you making me nervous.

—Your carnet, Dude, or I'll take you to the unit for lack of respect and disregard for rank!

—Shameless, and you talking about your sister!

—Your…!

—There you go, but stop it with your carnets already! My Spanish passport! And proud of it!

—Gerónimo Martín Pinzón. Born in Ha-va-na. See? What kind of a worm you are!

—Show me yours?

—*My what? My mimi? Because I'm not showing you my mimi, fucker, no way.*

—Your passport.

—Be gentle, Dude, you know where it hurts.

—Not your Cuban passport, no, daughter, the Spanish one, and stop talking like that, you used to pronounce the Z, like God commands.

—Ay, my Z is scarcer than toilet paper outside a hotel where you pay in currency.

—That's why I'm saying, let's go to Spain. Who wants to stay in a country where you can't even wipe your ass.

—How he loves shooting off his mouth about that!

—Come on, your Spanish passport!

—You wish. Here's my temporary cu-ba-no residence card.

—Yes, but issued to foreigners. Isabel de Bobadilla. Born in Seville, S-p-a-i-n. La Giraldilla, couldn't be more obvious than that.

—What'ya mean, Giraldilla? What nerve! Only Eusebio can call me Giraldilla.

—No, I was just saying, between you and me... Kidding around! And why do you put your mother's last name first?

—Because that's the only Spanish thing I have left: I can choose the order of my surnames. And you know, I'm going to propose that to the Federation so they can take it to People's Power. And I don't pronounce my Z because I don't want to, which is also why I'm not going back to Spain with you.

—Well, shit on the host. And I'm the worm. You know what I say? As long as you been on the Island, they aint gonna let you be Cuban if you don't drink rum.

—Don't spout off with me, old man, why you talking like that? No, you really bitch me out...

—Stop talking in Yoruba like that, talk to me Christian.

—Ay, old man, the next time you come from the Canaries why don't you bring me some white clothing? Skirts, handkerchiefs for my hair, an umbrella, shoes. A whole shitload to last me a year, because I want to make the saint.

—You want to do what? Come on, stop all this stuff, the day I least suspect I'm gonna find you licking yourself and singing that ditty they even put in the soup. How does it go? Sing it, come on.

—*I don't give an American fuck.*

—You gotta, cuz I'm your father.

—*Oh no, not that. Look, I've spent my money and that's not going anywhere.*

—Like I said, and the family don't float, you know. Not even your sister makes me so mad.

—Because you bring her things.

—And what's that gotta do with it?

—Because you know how to avoid arguments with her! Last time didn't you bring her condoms that don't tear and the morning after pill?

—Uhuh. But what I was saying. They just fired you from Havana Club for abstemious. So they probably gonna keep on denying you residence for the same thing. Cuz they use the most surreal excuses to hang up your papers.

—Not hang up, hold up. Talk pretty, old man, all these years on the Island and you still confuse Eleguá with the Virgin of the Macarena.

—And you confuse feeding yourself with stuffing yourself every day with a plate of rice with black beans.

—Not black beans. Frijoles. And I don't eat rice and beans every day.

—Because you work for the Historian's Office, but that's no reason to stay. Let's go to Spain. I don't think you understand that your residency is about to run out.

—A lie! Let's see. Oh my god!

—You've got fifteen days to get out. Just enough to show your sister Giraldilla's trade, that she already knows, because she's the real thing, even though I don't think about her that much, and to say goodbye to your lover.

—Don't talk about Eusebio like that.

—You act like a dead fly, but you hustle the tourists more than he does. That uncle scrounging around in the hotels. No, if that's the way it was, all you'd have to do is hold out your hand and the Euros would fall from the sky. And in the very crisis!

—You just talking to talk. I'm gonna ask for the extension.

—Come on now, not the MININT or the MINREX or any other ministry wants you on the Island.

—I'm not giving up. Forget that. The Office is above all the ministries, even the Ministry of the Interior and of Sugar.

—If it still exists, because everything here is very sweet, sickeningly sweet, but politics is a joke.

—Listen, Eusebio, my love, I need you to get me one of those letters, Immigration hasn't discovered that I am the symbol of the city. I mean excuse me, of The City. *This is my city, the problem is international.* Thank you, my love, Yes, tonight. At the Conqueror Suite in the hotel you gonna inaugurate.

—No, where I said, I mean Diego. Can I know why you insist on staying here?

—A person has her destiny in life. Mine is watching the horizon,

writing down the direction of the winds and welcoming the boats that enter the bay of San Cristobal of Havana.

—You telling me after all this time you still believe that fucker of a husband of yours is coming back. How dumb can you be, daughter!

—He be back. I know he be back. I know, it's been almost five centuries. But that's nothing. He drank from the Fountain of Youth.

—Dumber than dumb. But can't you see they all the same!

—You should know, cuz you're a man.

—You should know, cuz you say you're so Cuban.

—*How I love being from Havana.*

—Don't sing while I'm talking to you, and think about what you gonna say.

—He's coming back, Dude, he takes his time but I know he be back the same way he went! He told me I was *his mango, his caramel, his doll, how I love you, his Ve Ay Pee dancer, his little bit of sugar for his coffee.*

—I'm gonna tell you in your language: That nigger is a fucker and you're stupid. Understand?

—No, you really treat me bad, Papi....

—Not papi, or host. The guy you shoulda married was Hernando de Soto, he woulda been a good husband. But not you, you had to look at that black man who got you into bed before the honeymoon because that Spanish passport burned a hole in his hands.

—He not black. He brown.

—Black and a monk to boot. And you telling me you not like your sister. You twins, dammit, and I know you like I gave birth to you myself.

—Ummm.

—So you can tell me I act like a gringo.

—*You gotta go dancing.*

—Okay, and what if he don't come back?

—And who's tellin you I want to stay for him?

—For who, then?

—For nobody, fucker. For me. I just feel like staying. What do you care. It's my life!

—Well, sometime you think you want something and it's just that you don't know nothin else. And you do, but you've forgotten, so it's time you remember.

—*Not me, get it on with Puerto Rico,* cuz I got internet and I know what's happening in the world. Listen up, and this thing you have about sending me back to Spain?

—There's nothing wrong with a father worrying about his daughter's future.

—Listen here, didn't you just buy some expensive rum in Las Palmas?

—I did.

—And the owner of the shipyard isn't your jeba?

—Not really my jeba... What does that damned word mean anyway?

—And the owner of the building that gonna build a monument at the entrance to the port, aint he your buddy?

—I was godfather at his son's wedding. Speaking of that, he just got divorced. What you smiling about?

—And you say you don't have a nickel in your pocket.

I don't, but I'm a resourceful man. Daughter, I'm happy you concerned about your father but, why all the questions?

—Some nerve, you wanna hustle your own daughter! You want to get me on a ship so you can make me your slave. That's all.

—No, daughter. How come you think that about your father? Everything I do is for your good. It would never occur to me to make you drink rum against your will. If you want, you can appear on the label drinking honey. The binkini, it can be a swim suit. And the monument, the bargain of the century for you. Come on, do it with the cap. You can pose sitting down and without the cross so you don't get so tired. But you gotta whistle with the host when a Moroccan ship comes along.

—Drugs, noooo! Don't get me into drugs, at least I can pretend not to see over here.

—Drugs, what are you saying? By god!

—No trafficking in immigrants either.

—No, nothing like that. Everything legal. And I won't work for free. What's the minimum pay, for professionals? Okay, a little more, and don't get that look on your face, we've all done it from time to time. What more do you want? And keep on living on an Island, if that's what you like.

—I'm not listening. *Tell me how you've been, if you've found happiness.*

—Listen, sshhh. Shut up. Do you hear steps?

—Talk all you want, I'm not listening. *You crying in Miami, me living it up in Havana.*

—Isabel, don't sing so loud, I think someone's climbing the tower stairs.

—*I'll stay in Havana, because my Havana is a dream and even so, I changed owners.*

—Didn't I tell you? It's your sister. And she's coming with the mp4 stuck to her ear. Just like her.

—And what you saying?

—*It's here, the machine is here, it's here. It comes sweeping roads.*

—Don't play dumb, for sure you the one who told her to come. What you want, shameless one? Are you coming to take my tower too?

—*Stay where you are, cuz pain will become pleasure, and it's the same in the end.*

—No, my daughter, no! I'm here to say goodbye. And it's not an mp4. It's an mp15.

—*Lose your life, lose your home, lose everything but your soul.*

—Isabel, isn't that suitcase a little big to be taking to Varadero?

—And who says I'm going to Varadero?

—Where would you be going? If you never been anywhere but Old Havana.

—*Havana, beautiful Havana, your park is beautiful, your streets are beautiful, beautiful is your sea.*

—To Italy.

—Italy?

—Italy?

—That's right. With the owner of a new brand of Lambrusco wine.

—Now this really is for shit!

—*With the permission of the Zafiros and with all due respct... Oh, my Havana, I don't know if your sea wall is for fun or one long immigration office.*

—I shit on my dad! You breed crows and they'll take out your eyes.

—*Havana, beautiful Havana, your park is beautiful, your streets are beautiful, beautiful is your sea.*

Lima, January 2010

To my Havana, with love and pain

Darsi Fernández Maceira

Postscript

Subject: a little favor

Darsita:

Magnificent, joyous, pleasing...today's Café Dulce. I was surprised you and M. weren't there. Are you all right? In any case you were with me, in my heart, with good music....

Will you send me Manelic Ferret's email? I want to invite her to contribute to a wonderful book of Cuban women. And I would like to send her a strange poem I dedicated to her, although she ignores me outrageously. Another thing: Do you have Nelda Castillo's email? Irene Borges? I'm going to attach the invitation so you can suggest some genius I may not know.

A great hairy hug,
S... and Gala... (last night she spoke to me in a dream, as if it were the most natural thing)

Subject: Re: a little favor

Dear Sole:

I love your mood. And I'm so glad the Café Dulce was a success. The electricity went out at the office for almost two hours on Friday afternoon and everything was gloomy. I don't have the luxury of letting things pile up, and I have a lot to do since I was out for a few days with that crazy production of the 13th Street concert. So I was trying to get caught up so I'd be able to go to your Café Dulce for children, but it didn't happen, it was after six when I finished.

I've also been having strange dreams, some beautiful ones I'll tell you about for your collection. I don't think it's weird that Gala spoke to you. Coincidentally, last night I copied a poem by Virgilio Piñera dedicated to a woman friend, in which he says: *Love makes miracles and one of them is getting a dog to speak to its owner*, read it to Gala so she won't feel bad.

I'll go over my list of geniuses who have email and I'll call you this afternoon.

D

PS: On Friday I was at the premier of Enrique Pineda Barnet's film *Verde verde*. One could criticize a thousand things about its dramatic style, the script, the staging, the direction and almost everything else. But I was impressed with Pineda's eternal youth, how he can be so old and still be giving lessons in courage (form and content) to our prudish and boring young people. You know, I would like to write about that.

Subject: invitation

Dearest D.

Can I get you to write something about eternal youth or about whatever you want for the book I told you about? I'll explain when we see each other.

When you have time, call me so we can get together.

A kiss,
Sole

Subject: Re: invitation

How wonderful talking to you this morning. You were luminous and kind. Thank you.

Please, do you have Omar Pérez's email? I need to involve him as poet and translator in the project I was telling you about involving a concert on e .e. cummings' poetry.

I kiss your heart
Darsi

PS: I don't even want to think about what you proposed. Literary pretension is not my thing. I don't know what made me tell you about that sort of outburst. I didn't mention it, but Farah María was the one who provoked it. Yes...the same Farah María you thought of, the singer and model of the seventies. She plays a very curious role in the film, a symbol, one of the protagonist's more or less oblique conscience, the protagonist who ends up killing the other after having had sex with him. Farah María's face, older now, with hardly any makeup, is very suggestive. It's her fault. But forget it. I wouldn't think of it.

Subject: Oh mar

Darsita:

Here is Omar's email: habanazen@......... I'll trade it to you for Teresita Fernández's.

About the text, I don't want you to feel pressured. If it's easier for you, you could write a kind of report for the book, a notarized document, something of a judicial nature that is more familiar to you. That would be fantastic. Did you ever buy Graziella Pogolotti's book?

If you see stars shining, shine.

Your
Soleida

Subject: Oh mar

Sole:

I'm afraid Teresita Fernández doesn't have anything to do with such technology, but if she did have an email address it would be, without doubt, vinagrito@cubarte.cult.cu.

Thanks for Omar's email. I remembered it was something zen-like, but couldn't find it anywhere. He said yes to the project of translating and singing to cummings. I am happy but a bit overwhelmed, I don't know why I get involved in everything that seems interesting or challenging to me. That's why I don't want to commit to writing what you're asking for the book, and I'm even less enthusiastic about doing so in a formal or legal tone.

I bought you Pogolotti's book, but then I gave it to someone else who happened along. You can't put off visiting me for so long. I'll buy you another copy when I come across one. Or I could always lend you mine.

A kiss and a hug,
Darsi

PS: It's not that I feel offended at the idea that my participation in the women's book could be in the form of a report or a judgement or something of that sort. It might be the solution if I at least had the talent to write one of those. It must be that, since I have never been your usual bureaucrat, I've never had to write many reports, evaluations, declarations, opinions and that whole mess of such texts with which one might assume I am familiar. To do something like that, I'd have to try doubly hard, because I don't know how to write reports and even less reports disguised as literature.

Subject: maría gravina

Darsita:

Today I learned that María Gravina is very sick.

That was enough to make me feel low, but the loss of B. was terrible.

Love will make me grow a little more this year.

Sole

PS: Gala says: Martín, now you have a new little turtle, and she's on fire.... Her name is Josefina, Jose for short like you wanted.

Subject: Re: maría gravina

Good god. I hope it's not serious and that she gets better soon. Try to be calm and have good thoughts for her and for yourself.

I hope we see each other soon.... I have a lot of work, improvising all the time with Martín. Yesterday I told him to come by and pick up the little turtle Josefina (or Jose) but at the last minute I decided to drop her off.... I was tired and still had to decide what I was going to cook.

When you want, come for a while to look at the Havana Bay from this window.

A cloudy day kiss
D

PS: I try not to think of your proposal, but almost can't avoid it, despite all I'm doing. If I could write something, I'm almost positive Farah María would be the person, trying to enter the movie theater on opening night and finding a line of policemen, forming a sort of wall or barrier just beyond the Chaplin's terrace—I saw this with my own eyes—, an image much like that of Rocío García (she and her artwork are another character in the film).

So, Farah is an actress invited by the director and she tries to enter the theater but she's arrived late. There's some confusion, they've already closed the doors to invited guests and today's police don't recognize this Farah María as the woman for whom the police, captains, generals, and recruits of the seventies would have died. Maybe she remains outside the theater thinking about her life...about how, from having been a symbol of youth and beauty, she's become a symbol of sin or of sin's conscience.... Stop already, Sole, I don't know how to write...you should write it...author's rights don't protect ideas.

Subject: talismans

Sole,

The talismans you give us, what kind are they or what culture do they belong to?

PS: Let's stop talking about that. I'm not going to be able to write anything. The last time I tried, I left Farah María on 23rd Street, before the astonished and insulting gaze of all those policemen who think she's crazy, because she is an elderly woman talking about how she stopped Havana traffic with her figure, telling them she filmed Cuba's first video clip in a bikini, with a quartet called Los Meme. At a moment of calm—because the lobby of the theater has gone dark and no one is coming or going—she sings for a nearby group of policemen that song that makes her seem so sensual: *No me baño en el Malecón, porque en el agua hay un tiburón...*with her habitual saltiness... and the policemen begin to sing along with her. (Haha, at least I'm enjoying myself....)

I'm really busy, organizing a work trip, but I love you a lot,
D

Subject: Re: talismans

Rune talismans, they are Celtic in origin. Relatively unknown.

In fact, today is Monday, the day of Eleguá: wet your shell, place it in some little corner filled with light...so it will accompany you "well oiled." You must talk to it, tell it where you are going and what you want that trip, that pathway, to be like.

Promise not to torment me more with your possible collaboration. I got my hopes up, but I know you're busy. It's not fair.

Tell me if the guys who sold you that tuna are still around. I want to buy some more.

A dog's love!!!
Soleidar

Subject: trip

Thanks so much for understanding.

Maybe on my trip if I feel freer from tension to work on the story, fictional mini-biography or whatever you want to call what you're asking me to do, maybe then I'll have something for you on my return. Why can't I just tell you no, that I can't and don't know how to do it?

A warm embrace, full of love, see you when I get back.
Dar-si

PS: The worst thing is, I've imagined that the film *Verde verde* has ended and a mostly gay public is emerging from the theater, they're the ones who have been invited to the premier because of its subject matter and, just as you'd think, Farah María is supremely loved by that public, she's a kind of icon (it's curious, the Cuban woman who has provoked the greatest sentiments of macho possessiveness in our recent cultural history is, at the same time, a *queer* idol...).

The gays recognize her and begin to form a circle around her, cheering her...wanting to shake her hand...but she's just spent the hour and a half the film lasted putting on a show for those young policemen, who now think she is in danger and protect her from her fans, and in the middle of 23rd Street, in front of the movie house, a series of concentric circles form around her, with Farah María in the center. The first circle is made up of police, the gays are farther out and they are trying to get close to her. By this time, she's practically inaccessible.

Then she begins to sing: *Adios muchachos, compañeros de mi vida....* Hahahaha...

Subject: love

D,

How was your trip? Was it very short, or did it just seem that way to me? I'm very busy with the book, although I no longer resign myself to you not being in it.

The truth is, your idea about Farah and the film seemed to be gaining a resemblance to a detective story version of *La Bella de la Alhambra*, but I don't really know if it fits in the book.

Now it occurs to me that maybe we could select a part of our email correspondence on the subject, we might come up with an interesting text that is a metaphor or biography of our friendship. At least our virtual friendship.

I'll come by later to pick up the rice crackers and, if you have time, we'll talk.

An embrace,
Sol

Subject: Re: love

Sole,

Later I'll tell you about the trip that, fortunately, was short.

A while back I read a book by a Puerto Rican named Luis López Nieves. The book is structurally composed of emails and I couldn't tell you the genre: it's a thriller, it has suspense, it's philosophical, has history, genetics, anthropology...and it's very entertaining.

I don't think there would be anything original about publishing our emails. The last thing I need is to be in your book and for someone to accuse me of plagiarism, and that's the end of my career.

A kiss,
Dar

Subject: Re: Re: love

Dear Darsita:

Let's do this: you work on organizing it and then let me decide what to do with your text. I'm the one who had the idea (?), the anthologizer (?), and so I'm the one with the responsibility for this book. Numerous texts have come out of more or less manipulated correspondence (before and since there's been *email*); that writer you're talking about certainly doesn't have a patent on that type of text.

Manelic already sent me her collaboration, it seems like I was wrong about her thinking me full of shit.

We'll talk tomorrow, until then a hug,
Soleida

Sandra Ramy

My Work is You

Light gradually floods the stage and establishes an atmosphere of soft intensity. On both sides of the proscenium, creating a perspective of depth, there are two walls that enclose the space. I appear to one side and in the back, in profile, leaning forward a bit as if talking to a child, and with my hands together in front of me clapping out the rhythm as I sing:

Happy birthday, Sandra, on your day
May you spend it in health and happiness.
Many years of peace and harmony.
Happy birthday! Happy birthday! Happy birthday!

I fill my lungs with air and blow into the small cavity between my palms, filling them like one would blow out a birthday candle, and transforming it into a closed box.

I become a hen. I do so following specific rules: look for a good place, protect myself, settle in. The direction of my head and gaze precede all other movements. My hands and what they have in them are hidden behind my back, so it's only possible to see my arms and elbows flapping the way they do when we want to simulate a hen. Nevertheless, it's not an imitation: it's about conveying something through evocative actions.

—*The egg is something we must care for. That's why the hen is the egg's disguise.* (photo of a hen) *The hen exists* (I show an eye) *so the egg can travel through time. You must say the hen's egg.* (I turn my head, showing my other eye) *If you only say the egg, it's all over and the world remains naked* (I look at myself).

As for the hen's body, it is the most important proof that the egg doesn't exist. (my hands remain above my head, still containing air within

them, and come down slowly) *It's enough to look at the hen's body for it to be obvious that the egg is* (my hands open suddenly and naturally, as if nothing had ever been hidden in them) *impossible.*

Nothing, I show everyone I have nothing, not in my hands, not under my arms, not on my back, not under my skin, nothing at all resembling an egg. I search features of my anatomy, signs that distinguish me, also the presence of others on my body, from my head down to where I am poking at a toe with my right index finger. This is all I can do, search myself, search myself, search myself....

The hen's prejudices against the impossible egg are mine when I don't give in. Those who believe me possess themselves. The I is such an indelible part of them they can't even go on pronouncing the word...egg. But who know if this was what the...egg needed. The egg is the hen's great sacrifice (I signal the bags under my eyes) *The egg is the cross the hen carries through life* (with both hands I deliver blows to my shoulders that labor to carry such weight). *The egg is* (I raise my arms and look to the sky) *the hen's unachievable dream. To be a hen is the hen's survival, etcetera, etcetera, eggcetera, eggcetera, eggce, egg, egg, egg, egg....*

I let my arms fall, I walk on arms and legs, grabbing at the floor and letting the word *egg* escape as if it had a life of its own. I bump into the wall, suddenly noticing it is there. I am very close to it, I can't see anything but the wall and the wall gives me back my consciousness of myself. Facing it, I remember a song from my childhood:

> *Little spring butterfly*
> *winged soul fluttering here and there.*
> *Through the gardens of my fantasy*
> *through the gardens of my fantasy*
> *like a whisper of fleeting love...*

The melody of the accompanying violin continues as I silently press the wall's hardness into my body, compact like a stone that moves with brief interruptions. I disappear from the audience's view while the melody can still be heard and behind it a rhythmic base that

gradually slows as I return, wearing high shoes with red heels like the ornament in my hair.

I approach the light, and look at the faces of the people who are waiting for me, waiting eagerly. The show must go on. I begin to sing a peasant song. As I do, I acknowledge my shame, displayed in the movement of my feet, one heel falls off, I shake both feet behind me, and scratch the ground in a gesture of giving birth. It is a scene about expectations and about everything one does to win approval. *Dancing the son, I break my heart....* The melody is slow, dense, as I let my body be carried by moving my weight from one foot to the other, forward, to one side, back, to one side. *Dancing the son, I break my heart....* My feet in their shoes planted on the floor, strong, sustaining the movement of my torso. *Dancing the son, I break my heart.* The circle concentrates in the pelvic area and gains in velocity as the movement slows. *The hen has a rich internal life.* The circular pelvic movement becomes more intense. *The hen's internal life is about acting....* She stops abruptly and nods her head as she says: ... *as if it understood.* I display my ambivalence, my vulnerability. To accept, agree, go back in her box. Proud and ready. Only at a certain point my feet, my shoes, fail to respond, engaging me in a ridiculous dance that causes me to stumble, pretend, get up and fall again, until finally, exhausted, I take my shoes off and let my feet come in contact with the floor. This contact deflates me and allows me to feel the weight of my bones, my skeleton. I look out at the audience again, I draw closer and, letting my head wobble back and forth and with my shoes in my hands, ask one of those sitting there: *Do you know how to say no?*[14]

On a wall the image of a hen walking among people in the street appears, accompanied by the melody from *The Death of the Swan*, by C. Saint-Saëns. The hen looks in astonishment at the human construction. Estranged from, and incomprehensible to, everyone. The music stops. The projection ends. Silence.

To move in silence, following the rhythm that comes from one's own focus, is a uniquely subtle experience. In silence everyone, observers and actors alike, construct the action. The body is an open door

14. Dialog with the story "The Hen and the Egg," by Clarice Lispector.

through which a storm brews. Territory upon which the meeting of inside and out takes place. Movement is reaction, lightning. The walls, like the body, contain, conform, hide. They also paralyze, and in one stroke force recognition.

It is a delicate task to create a self-portrait in action, one that simultaneously functions as an exercise in understanding oneself and an object of reflection for others. Two doors and several questions open before me: "How to paint myself? How to give myself to the events that have shaped me, and which instruments bring them to life? And finally, what in all that may be of interest or use to the theatergoer who hopes to receive food for her own life? Even when, in some cases, she may not be conscious of the quest.

The theatrical event and artistic personality, for some time now, are extremely uncomfortable for me. I'm not at all sure about theater, neither do I know if it's important that it be useful. I have developed an intimate relationship with movement and dance, and it is a fundamental relationship in my life; but the audience: what role does it have? It is here, where these two impulses come together, where I find once again the departure point, the relationship. This is the thing, this is the egg.

To make a mirror rather than a portrait. A mirror in which I may come in contact with areas that are both difficult and common to all. To find myself and where they find themselves. In the exercise, perhaps we find each other.

Questions: What image do you create for others? What image do you have of yourself? What words define you? What object are you, that is to say, of what use? What animal, song? What are your fears? Your hidden places? Features of your anatomy and activity in which you find others. In short, what do you do? What are your favorite lies?

About the Authors:

Caridad Atencio (Havana, 1963) has published poetry, essays and criticism. Among her books: *Los cursos imantados* (2000), *La sucesión* (2004) and *El libro de los sentidos* (National Literary Critics Prize, 2010); *La saga crítica de* Ismaelillo (2008) and *Los cuadernos de apuntes de José Martí o la legitimación de la escritura* (2012). Most fervent desire: *About this, one can neither content oneself with being selfish nor educated nor popular. Let there be no war. I can give thanks for many things, but one of the most important is being the daughter of good, decent and sensitive parents.*

Ruth Behar (Havana, 1956) teaches anthropology at the University of Michigan. Among her books of poetry and prose: *Bridges to Cuba* (editor, 1995), *Translated Woman: Crossing the Border with Esperanza's Story* (1993), *An Island Called Home: Returning to Jewish Cuba* (2007), and *Traveling Heavy: A Memoir in Between Journeys* (2013). Ediciones Vigía in Matanzas published her *Poemas que vuelven a Cuba*, *Todo lo que guardé*, and *La Cortada*. In 2002 she premiered *Adio Kerida*, a documentary about the search for identity among Sephardic Jews with roots in Cuba. Most fervent desire: *Not to lose my memory. I am grateful for everything I can remember.*

Teresita Burgos Benavides (Matanzas, 1954) is a poet, dramatist and writer of fiction. Poetry collections: *Cuando la luna se sienta en el limonero* (1984, 2003), *Revelaciones* (1987), *Junto al ceremonial nostálgico de los hornos* (1989), and *Días muertos de una isla* (soon to be released). *Habitantes de la penumbra* (2005) is a novel. *Libro blanco* (2009) is a book of poetic prose. She heads the Eliseo Diego Experimental Workshop of Literary Creation, and writes radio scripts on universal literature. Most fervent desire: *To be in the precise spot where my people come together. Thanks to life: for not abandoning me along the way.*

Damaris Calderón (Havana, 1967) has published in Cuba, Chile and Mexico. Among her books: *Sílabas. Ecce Homo, El remoto país imposible, Duro de roer, Los amores del mal, Parloteo de sombra* and *Las pulsaciones de la derrota*. Her work has been translated into various languages. She won a Guggenheim Fellowship in 2011. *I am thinking about a doorway in Havana. In the eighties. A building covered with scaffolding. It is raining. I am cold and hungry. I have a few of my poems in my pocket and feel I am immortal [...] I love a woman who loves me. I am ferocious, delicate, brutal and believe poetry is the only thing that matters. I am grateful to life, to this moment of remembrance, of knowing who I am.* Most fervent desire: *if I could only find the way back.*

Irela Casañas Hijuelos (Santiago de Cuba, 1980) studied sociology at the University of Oriente, Cuba. She has published poems and essays in many Cuban magazines. Among her books: *Manual del triunfo* (2006) and *Testimonio del margen* (2011). *It may seem naïve or clichéd, but my fervent desire is that the society in which I live be authentically happy. I give thanks because my feet are not completely on the ground and because I know many people who have the same "problem."*

Adelaida de Juan (Havana, 1931) has published many works in the fields of essay and art criticism. Outstanding among these: *Pintura y grabado coloniales cubanos: contribución a su estudio* (1974), *Hacerse el Bobo de Abela, Historia de Cuba. Las artes plásticas en Cuba, Caricatura de la República*, and *José Martí: imagen crítica y mercado de arte*. She is a Professor Emerita at the University of Havana. She was awarded the Bibliography of Art Criticism Prize by Mexico's Fondo de Cultura Económica in 1964, and the National Guy Pérez Cisneros Prize in art criticism for a lifetime's work. *I want to keep on working. I give "thanks to life."*

Darsi Fernández Maceira (Havana, 1966) is an attorney and cultural promotor. She has produced concerts by artistic groups such as Calle 13, Habana Abierta, Interactivo, Yusa and Lenine, among others. She has curated art exhibitions and written music criticism and interviews

in the Cuban press. *I want to live and die in peace. I am grateful for having lived in this country at this time.*

Mylene Fernández Pintado (Havana, 1963) won the David Prize for Short Story in 1998 with *Anhedonia,* the Italo Calvino Prize in 2002, and the National Literary Critics Prize in 2003 for *Otras plegarias atendidas.* Other works are *Little Woman in Blue Jeans* (2008), *Infiel y otras historias* (2009), and *La esquina del mundo* (2011). *Giordano Bruno said that the Earth had a soul and the stars were angels. I want us not to harm that soul which contains us, and which we carry within. I give thanks to everyone who, in the fields of art, science, theology, and politics... dedicate their time and energy so the world will more just.*

Manelic R. Ferret (Santiago de Cuba, 1961) studied Philology at the University of Oriente, Cuba. *Libro del buey* (Calendario de Poesía Prize, 1998). A composer and musical interpreter, she wrote for *Cubaneo* (one of the first alternative magazines in Havana in the 1990s) before going to live in Barcelona. Her fervent desire: *To return and leave again and return.... Thanks for the music.*

Lourdes González Herrero (Holguin, 1952) is "incessant" in her field: she runs a publishing house, a production center, her home, her work, and herself; she edits a newspaper and journal; and she teaches poetry (sic). Among her recent books of poetry and narrative: *Afuera sangran los caballos, La sombra del paisaje, El hijo de la arpista, El amanuense. My fervent desire: to keep my moral integrity. I give thanks to life for allowing me to do so.*

Charo Guerra (Limonar, Matanzas, 1962) is a poet and fiction writer. Books of poetry: *Un sitio bajo el cielo* (1991), *Los inocentes* (1963), *Vámonos a Icaria* (1998) and *Luna de los pobres* (2011); short story collection: *Pasajes de la vida breve* (2007). *Mi fervent desire: to possess, in any circumstance, the joy of living. I give thanks in my life that I enjoy it and share that joy.*

Georgina Filomena Herrera Cárdenas (Matanzas, 1936). After *GH* (1962), some of her other poetry collections survive: *Gentes y cosas, Grande es el tiempo, Granos de sol y luna, Gustadas sensaciones, Golpeando la memoria, Gatos y liebres, Gracias a la muerte*, and numerus radio novels. She has done sociological studies on women, black women in particular. She has been awarded the Distinction for National Culture (Cuba), Buenaventura tiene la Palabra (Colombia) and the Cuautlicue Statuette for Iberoamerican Women (Mexico), among others. *I want to be vital, coherent, as I have been up to now. I give thanks for the way I am and the way I live, because it is an unending luxury to listen more than to speak.*

Amalia Iduate Gómez (Havana, 1971) studied philosophy, graphic design, and composition. She designed the cover of this volume *Mi fervent desire: To play the piano. Thanks for the seashell's calm, and for containing a single heart.*

Yannis Lobaina (Baracoa, 1979) is involved in film production. She has published stories in *Paralelo Sur* and *Isliada* (digital), as well as in the anthology *Las cuenta cuentos* (2012). *Despedida*, her first book of narrative, was published in Barcelona. *My fervent desire, right now, is not to lose my ability to believe in human beings. I give thanks to all those who respect my life decisions.*

Zurelys López Amaya (Havana, 1967) is a poet. Her books include *Pactos con la sombra* (2009, 2010) and *Rebaños* (2010). She was a finalist in the Los Odres de Murcia international literature contest (Spain). *My fervent desire is to remain healthy so I can go on dreaming and living with the people I love. I give thanks for my health so far, and to have given birth to my daughter Lisandra.*

Marcela López Gravina (Montevideo, 1967) is an adopted daughter of Cuba, living in Alamar. She studied sociology at the University of Havana. She possesses a writer's daily persistence and pens transgeneric lines in cyberspace. *I fervently desire to keep on desiring, and that my world not dissolve in that which lies ahead. Thanks to life for all those*

who started me on my path, those I loved and who loved me unconditionally; for the night I gave birth; for literature, dogs and fish, and for the long road that brought me to the embrace of the man I love today....

Margarita Mateo Palma (Havana, 1950) holds a Ph.D. in Literary Sciences and is a member of the Cuban Academy of Language. She has won the National Literary Critics Prize five times. Most important works: *Ella escribía poscrítica* (1995 and 2006), *Paradiso: la aventura mítica* (Alejo Carpentier Prize, 2001), *El palacio del pavorreal: el viaje mítico* (UNEAC's Enrique José Varona Prize, 2006), and a novel, *Desde los blancos manicomios* (Alejo Carpentier Prize, 2008). *My fervent desire: is a secret. For what am I grateful? Almost everything. I spend my life giving thanks.*

Nara Mansur Cao (Havana, 1969). Her books of poetry and theater include: *Mañana es cuando estoy despierta* (2000), *Un ejercicio al aire libre* (2004), *Manualidades* (Nicolás Guillén National Poetry Prize, 2011) and *Desdramatizándome. Cuatro poemas para el teatro* (National Literary Critics Prize, 2011). Fervent desire: *Happiness for those I love, the revolution of the revolution of the revolution in Cuba, and peace and social justice for the world. I am grateful to be part of a collective project, and to be able to work in a field I love. I give thanks to those who respect me for who I am, to those who love me, to those who love one another and to those I love.*

Jamila Medina Ríos (Holguín, 1981) is a poet and essayist. In poetry: *Huecos de araña* (David Prize, 2008), *Primaveras cortadas* (2013), and *Del corazón de la col y otras mentiras* (2013). In narrative: *Ratas en la alta noche* (2011). In essay: *Diseminaciones de Calvert Casey* (Alejo Carpentier Prize, 2012). *I wanted to thank JAAD, who connected my writing with that of CC. I would like to find myself with Gianni-Gianni, sitting on CC's lost grave in the Campo de Verano Cemetery. I always give thanks when a fervent desire embraces me.*

Lizabel Mónica (Havana, 1981) is the founder of the digital multidisciplinary project *Desliz*. She has published poems, stories, essays and

art criticism in national and international magazines. She is currently working on a novel, *Tim sin Tina*, and a collection of poems, *Nudo*. Involved in research linking literature, the arts, and digital media, she is studying for her doctorate at Princeton University. *I give thanks to my family, from which I have always received inspiration in my life and work.* Fervent desire: *To one day make mine Pavese's phrase:* the world's only joy is beginning.

Cirenaica Moreira (Havana, 1969) studied Theater Arts at the Higher Institute of Art. One-person and collective exhibitions of her work at the Couturier Gallery in Los Angeles, the Alida Anderson Project in Potomac, the Metropolitan Pavilion in New York, and the Gedok Galerie in Munich. She gave a talk at the National Geographic Magazine Seminar in 2012. Her work is in the collections of the National Museum of Bellas Artes in Havana, Le Filles du Calvaire Gallerie in Paris, the Fundación Arte Viva in Rio de Janeiro, the Art Museum of the University of Virginia, and the Jordan Schniczer Museum of Art in Oregon. *I wish that nothing and no one ever hurts my daughter, and I give thanks that it be that way, as well as for creativity, laughter and friendship.*

Andriana Normand (Berlin, 1976). In 2007 she published *Photomatum*, a book of short texts. She writes: *I want to live intensely. I want to thank life for all my loves, especially those of my mother and daughter, who are my greatest good.*

Dazra Novak (Quebec, 1978) studied history at the University of Havana. In 2007, she won the Pinos Nuevos Prize for her book of short stories *Cuerpo Reservado* (2008). She received the David Prize in 2007 and a special prize given by Cabeza de Zanahoria for another book of short stories, *Cuerpo Público* (2009). In 2010 she won the Fronesis Scholarship for Novel Writing, and in 2011 UNEAC's Cirilo Villaverde prize for her novel *Making Of* (2012). Fervent desire: *To explore Paris while reading* Rayuela. *I give thanks on this Caribbean island for the possibility of having the sea everyday.*

Gertrudis Ortiz (Sancti Spíritus, 1951) has published in anthologies, magazines and other media. A book of her stories is *Estoy despierta* (1990). Some of her plays have been produced. *I will keep my most fervent desire to myself. Each day and night I give thanks that I am the mother and grandmother of two precious girls.*

Basilia Papastamatíu (Buenos Aires, 1940) has lived in Havana since 1969. Her books include: *El pensamiento común, Qué ensueños los envuelven, Paisaje habitual, Allí donde, Dónde estábamos entonces, Espectáculo privado, Interpretación de la historia* (collected poems) and *Cuando ya el paisaje es otro.* Her *La Diana de Montemayor*, translated by Severo Sarduy, was staged at a Paris Art Biennial. She has directed the literary magazines *Airón* (Argentina, in the 1970s) and *La Letra del Escriba* (Havana, currently). She has been awarded the National Literary Critics Prize and a Distinction for Cuban Culture. Her work has been translated and published in Latin America and Europe. *What do I most desire? That we have more justice and love for one another. What do I give thanks for in my life? The opportunity to keep on experiencing it.*

Azucena Isabel Plasencia (Havana, 1946) is a member of the Cuban Association of Film Press, a section of FIPRESCI, and of the Union of Writers and Artists of Cuba. She has judged a variety of film festivals, among them Havana's International Festival of New Latin American Film. *I want my country to achieve economic and political stability so it can guarantee its people's personal and spiritual development in line with the changes that have taken place in the world. I am grateful for my two daughters, Lizabel and Lía, who are supportive, faithful friends, lovers of justice, good literature, all kinds of music and poetry without end.*

Olga Marta Pérez (Matanzas, 1952) has worked for years in the field of children's literature, and has several of her own children's books: *Papatino y Mamagorda, La Maga Maguísima, Traviesos de la noche* (all short stories); two novels: *Las sombras andan solas* and *Declarado desierto*; and poetry collected in: *Tricolor* (co-authored with Vivien

Acosta), *Tres lunas, Desde el cristal* and *Entre la luna y el agua.* Fervent desire: *To be happy, and I will always be grateful to be left alone.*

Gina Picart (Havana, 1956) has books in the genres of narrative and essay: *La poza del ángel* (David Science Fiction Prize, 1990), *El druida, Malevolgia, La ciudad de los muertos, Historias celtas, La poética del signo como voluntad y representación* (Luis Rogelio Nogueras Essay Prize, 2005), *Pasifae,* and *La casa del alibi.* Fervent desire: *Eternity. For what would I give thanks in my life: my daughter and my talent for language.*

Sandra Ramy (Havana, 1976). Has worked, on and off the Island, with contemporary choreographers and dance and theater companies. Teaches courses for writers, choreographers and dancers. Founded and directs the dance project *S Estudio,* an open creative space for children and adults without academic training. *I am grateful to have met some people early on who opened a crack in the floor upon which I walked, and helped me become familiar with the earth. I want my son Pablo to nurture his intuition and believe in himself.*

Legna Rodríguez Iglesias (Camagüey, 1984) is the author of *Ne me quitte pas, Qué te sucede, belleza, Dos uno cero* (selection of stories and poemas, 2011), *Mayonesa bien brillante* (novel), and the poetry collections *Tregua fecunda, Chupar la piedra* and *El momento perfecto.* She was awarded the Julio Cortázar Iberoamerican Short Story Prize in 2011. *What I want is to see you again, just for a moment, and then, when I do, thank you for my eyes. For the fire in the kitchen, the water in the fountain, and the pillow on the couch. And thank you, thank you, for saying it.*

Reina María Rodríguez (Havana, 1952) is a philologist. Numerous books of her poetry and prose have been published in Cuba, Europe and America, among them: *Cuando una mujer no duerme, En la arena de Padua, Páramos, Para un cordero blanco, La foto del invernadero, Te daré de comer como a los pájaros, Bosque negro, Violet Island y otros poemas, Variedades de Galiano, Las fotos de la señora Loss* and *Otras mitologías.* She won the Casa de las Américas Prize in 1984 and 1998. Her work

was awarded the Italo Calvino Novel Prize in 2005. On various occasions, she has been the recipient of Cuba's National Literature Prize. She holds France's Order of Arts and Letters (1999). Her work has been translated into several languages. Most fervent desire: *That we find one another. I am grateful to still have my mother with me.*

Laura Ruiz Montes (Matanzas, 1966) is the author of several poetry collections, including *Queda escrito, La sombra de los otros, Lo que fue la ciudad de mis sueños* (2000), *El camino sobre las aguas, A qué país volver, Los frutos ácidos* (National Literary Critics Prize 2008), and *Otro retorno al país natal.* Other works include *A Ciegas* (theater), *Hoy es domingo y mañana también* (children's novela) and *A la entrada y a la salida* (essays on several black female protagonists in Caribbean novels). Fervent desire: *That my daughter will always be well. For what do I give thanks? For life.*

Rocío Santillana (Lima, 1967) works in video art and writes scripts for television films and series. Her *Erocéntrica Poesía Inconsecuente,* was presented in Havana. She is a recipient of the Bioy Casares Short Story Prize (2010). Fervent desire: *To return to Havana. For what do I give thanks: infinite thanks for having been surrounded by people with clear and generous souls who have enriched my life. I would be happy if I am able to give them back the best of myself.*

Lía Villares (Havana, 1984) studied guitar at the Amadeo Roldán Music Conservatory and composition at the Higher Institute of Art. She is self-taught in photography and audiovisual arts. Website: http://habanemia.blogspot.com. *My fervent desire is to be with my most beloved family and close friends. To be with them on an island of dreams, that doesn't resemble, or hardly resembles, ours, and not to think about the climate or anything else. I give thanks all the time, even just "because." That's how one let's life lead one, and not the other way around.*

About the Editor:

Soleida Ríos (Santiago de Cuba, 1950). Among her books, the most important are *Poesía infiel* (Young Cuban Poets, 1989), *El libro roto* (1994, 2002), *Libro cero* (1999), *El texto sucio* (1999), *Fuga. Antología personal* (2004), *Secadero* (2009), *Escritos al revés* (2009, 2012, National Literary Critics Prize), *Aquí pongamos un silencio* (2010), *Estrías* (Nicolás Guillén National Poetry Prize, 2013, 2013), and two books of dreams (1999, 2011). Her *A wa nilé* is soon to be published. *I want to plant a forest of Cuban poetry, a real forest (one tree for every poet, living or dead) that can give us refuge, another way of breathing. I give thanks for this life, on this earth, which is not by chance.*

About the Translator:

Margaret Randall (New York, 1936) lived in Cuba from 1969 through 1980 and returns often. In addition to her own literary production (poetry, essay, oral history), she has translated a great deal of Cuban work. Among it: *Breaking the Silences: 20ᵗʰ Century Poetry by Cuban Women* (2982), *Only the Road / Solo el camino: Eight Decades of Cuban Poetry* (2016), *Diapositivas / Transparencies* by Laura Ruiz Montes, *trillos precipicios concurrencias* by Alfredo Zaldívar (2017), *What the Vampire Told Them* by Chely Lima (2017), and books by Israel Domínguez, Yanira Marimón, Reynaldo García Blanco, and Teresa Melo (forthcoming).

In 2017 Margaret was awarded the Medal of Literary Merit by Literatura en el Bravo, Festival Internacional Chihuahua, Ciudad Juárez.

Wings Press was founded in 1975 by Joanie Whitebird and Joseph F. Lomax, both deceased, as "an informal association of artists and cultural mythologists dedicated to the preservation of the literature of the nation of Texas." Publisher, editor and designer since 1995, Bryce Milligan is honored to carry on and expand that mission to include the finest in American writing— meaning all of the Americas, without commercial considerations clouding the decision to publish or not to publish.

Wings Press intends to produce multi-cultural books, chapbooks, ebooks, recordings and broadsides that enlighten the human spirit and enliven the mind. Everyone ever associated with Wings has been or is a writer, and we know well that writing is a transformational art form capable of changing the world, primarily by allowing us to glimpse something of each other's souls. We believe that good writing is innovative, insightful, and interesting. But most of all it is honest. As Bob Dylan put it, "To live outside the law, you must be honest."

Likewise, Wings Press is committed to treating the planet itself as a partner. Thus the press uses as much recycled material as possible, from the paper on which the books are printed to the boxes in which they are shipped.

As Robert Dana wrote in *Against the Grain*, "Small press publishing is personal publishing. In essence, it's a matter of personal vision, personal taste and courage, and personal friendships." Welcome to our world.

Colophon

This first English edition of *The Oval Portrait*, edited by Soleida Ríos and translated by Margaret Randall, has been printed on 55 pound Edwards Brothers "natural" paper containing a percentage of recycled fiber. Titles have been set in "Chaucer" type, the text in Adobe Caslon type. This book was designed by Bryce Milligan.

On-line catalogue and ordering:
www.wingspress.com
Wings Press titles are distributed to the trade by the
Independent Publishers Group
www.ipgbook.com
and in Europe by Gazelle
www.gazellebookservices.co.uk

Also available as an ebook.